DANIEL HARTJOY
PRESENTS

The WEALTH BUILDER *Lifestyle* WORKBOOK

DESIGN YOUR LIFESTYLE OF **PERPETUAL AND EXPONENTIAL** WEALTH CREATION

How The Other 99% Can Get Rich

Methods For Mastery, Inc.

Methods For Mastery, Inc.
PO Box 904
Wauna, WA 98395

Copyright © 2014 by Daniel Hartjoy

All rights reserved. No part of this publication may be reproduced, distributed, stored, or transmitted in any form or by any means, including in a database or retrieval system, without the prior written permission of the publisher.

www.WealthBuilderLifestyle.com

This publication contains the opinions and ideas of the author. It is designed to provide competent and reliable information regarding the subject matter covered. The strategies in this book may not be suitable for every individual. Furthermore, it is sold with the understanding that neither the author nor the publisher are providing legal (financial or other) advice. If legal assistance is required, the services of a professional should be sought. The author and publisher specifically disclaim any liability that is incurred from the use or application of the contents of this book. No particular results are guaranteed or warranted by using the information contained within.

This book is a nonfictional work. Names and places have been changed to protect the privacy of all individuals. Any resulting resemblance to persons living or dead is entirely coincidental and unintentional. The events and situations are true.

Printed in the United States of America

First edition 2014

ISBN: 978-0-9905072-1-5

Dedicated to those who go the extra mile to figure out what is holding them back, and then conquer it.

Contents

Acknowledgements 1
Introduction 3
Your Commitment 5
    THE REALITIES OF WEALTH TODAY 7
A Few Points To Consider 9
Get This 11
Four Keys to Being Rich 13
Only One Way to be Wealthy 15
Life Cycles Affect and Influence Everything 21
The Value of a Dollar 25
    PART ONE: CURRENT WEALTH STATUS 31
Financial Status Test 33
Spending 37
Income 39
Debt 41
Savings and Investments 43
Financial Security Cushion 45
Current Net Worth 47
Retirement Progress Chart 49
Meeting Needs 51

PART TWO: TWELVE MONTH REBALANCE 53

Risk Considerations 55
The Bomb - Income Allocations 57
Bad Habit Assessment 65
Investing Habits 67
Financial Security Insurance 69
Spending Alignment 77
Debt Reduction and Investments 81
Career Fast-Tracking 89
Career Action Plan 113
Housing 119
Rebalance Blueprint 137

PART THREE: WEALTH BUILDER ESSENTIALS 151

Investing 101 153
Personal Finance is Your Business 163
Financial Feng Shui: Your Environment 165
Your Image 169
Your Focus 173
Live in the Moment: Spend in the Past or Future 175
Intellectualizing Your Money Habits 177
Asset Allocations Simplified 181
Money-Wise Auto-Buying Guide 185
Luxury Purchase Analysis Tool 193
"Beat the Bank" Homeownership 197

CONCLUSION 203

Successfully Achieving Goals 205
Gratitude and Contribution 207
Money Mentor for Kids 209
Closing Thoughts 217

ACKNOWLEDGEMENTS

I want to extend my sincerest thanks to all the editing, publishing, production and creative staff that allow a book like this to come together. Without the help from all these essential people, this book would never have come to exist.

Less recognized, but every bit as essential are all of those who have struggled to figure out and get ahead in the wealth building game. You are the motivating force behind my desire to create and bring this book to life. It is all of you that inspired and provided the energy necessary for me to persevere and bring this resource to market. Now it is available for everyone who needs the answers that were previously not available to them in any format, let alone one they could understand and successfully use.

Lastly, to all of you who have used these methods and provided me with so much positive feedback about your results and the benefits these changes have made in your lives, thanks! That feedback and the generous words confirm that all the effort and work was well worth it.

INTRODUCTION

Building wealth is a lifelong pursuit, although it must be constant, it doesn't have to be complicated. The Wealth Builder Lifestyle is based on making good wealth building decisions your habitual behavior. Most people gamble with their financial fate by making numerous money decisions everyday with no plan or real understanding about how money works. This leads many to a life of frustration and lackluster financial success, if any success at all.

About This Workbook

To truly master anything in life takes time and continual improvement. All the strategies in this workbook are things anyone can and should learn and use. Your success will be determined by how well you not only intellectually understand these strategies, but also learn to incorporate them into your life and daily habits. This workbook is a companion to The WEALTH BUILDER *Lifestyle*: AN UNCOMMON GUIDE *ANYONE CAN USE* TO BUILD WEALTH AND LIVE A RECESSION READY LIFE book. This is a large-scale edition providing larger, easier to use worksheets and abbreviated versions of the strategies and philosophies covered in full within the book.

Life is a constant journey of learning and growing, so is your financial education. To maximize your wealth building potential use this workbook annually to create next year's financial strategy. This will allow you to check in on your progress, put focus on the areas you struggle with and strategize to make the most out of the next twelve months.

It's easy for people to look at these concepts and think they understand them and get it. Then two days later, they will be making a money decision that totally violates what they were sure they understood. This is very typical for people that have yet to master money and will destroy their chances of ever reaching millionaire status. We are trying to break bad financial habits that have been deeply ingrained in us for years.

It would be great to think financial mastery is a one and done proposition, but it's not. If you master the strategies in this system, you will build substantial wealth over your lifetime. Don't be one of those people on a constant pursuit of the next great money making secret who never takes the time to master anything they find. Everything you need is right here, just be realistic about what it will take to master it. Review this material annually and anytime you are making big money moves. If every year you pick up and make a few more of these skills a part of your daily lifestyle, you will soon master the art of perpetual and exponential wealth creation.

YOUR COMMITMENT

Nobody owes us anything. We all must take responsibility for our own financial well being.

Today, the average American has less than $3,800 in savings and twenty five percent of Americans have *nothing* in savings. Most have no idea what their net worth is, how much debt they're in, or how much wealth they will need to maintain a decent standard of living when they retire. You will soon be able to answer all those questions with certainty and have a strategic plan to get you exactly where you want to be.

Retirement may be a long ways away, but how you **choose** to live today will determine how you **have** to live in those later years. Use the Wealth Builder Lifestyle method to ensure that you can live life to the fullest now and have certainty that you will retire in comfort. Later is not the time to take action. Being passive today can ultimately leave you helpless and at the mercy of others when you are the most vulnerable. Nobody should allow themselves to get boxed into that situation, especially since when that time comes you may not even be physically capable of changing your situation. You can easily avoid being put in that devastating scenario. The solutions are simple and achievable by anyone, you just have to decide to take the necessary steps.

This is easier than you probably believe. And surprisingly, it's available to almost anyone who is willing to apply the simple principles outlined within. The real reason the rich keep getting richer and the poor keep getting poorer is because the rich prosper off of the concepts outlined here, while the poor have either never been exposed to them or destroy their chances for success by accepting the belief that it won't work for them. Once someone says, "I can't," and accepts that statement as true, all hope is lost and they will never even try to turn the doorknob of the door standing between them and success. Even an unlocked door will remain an impenetrable barrier to someone who never even bothers to try turning the knob. The key to your financial success is right here: open the door and come inside!

When you are ready to commit to yourself—to make sure you can be secure, thrive, and prosper from today on through the end of your time—put it in ink and let's get started. It's real easy to just think or say something, but not as easy to actually do it. If you are ready to make a real decision and secure a great future for yourself, commit to it in writing as your pledge to follow through with consistent and focused action.

My Commitment

Name: _____

Write a compelling statement about why you will complete this course. State it in the positive and be sure to include the outcomes that are the most important to you to achieve!

I'm committed to completing this course because:

_____

_____

_____

_____

_____

_____

_____

_____

_____

Date I Decided to Live a Rich Life and Die Wealthy:

Started on: _____/_____/_____

Date I Finished This Course and Fulfilled My Commitment:

Completed on: _____/_____/_____

"Wealth is created by a lifestyle, not an income."

- Daniel Hartjoy

THE REALITIES OF WEALTH TODAY

A FEW POINTS TO CONSIDER

The average net worth at age 65 in the US is less than $200,000, this average means there are many who are below that and some well below. In a time when the cost of getting by is rising extremely fast, being average or god forbid below average, is a scary and more likely proposition. I hope as a reader of this book you are someone who is willing to commit to taking the actions necessary to exceed well beyond average. Ponder these following questions for a few moments while you think about your current life status.

Are you at the level of wealth you expected you would be by your age? Looking back over the last five years, do you feel like you have things figured out and are growing your wealth adequately to ensure you reach your life and retirement goals? Do you enjoy your work and look forward to going to work every day? Do you have the lifestyle and luxuries you desire?

I hope your answers to these questions are all yes. If they're not, just keep in mind that almost everything in life is changeable if you're willing to learn how and then actually make some changes in your actions.

To succeed in wealth building you need to focus on two things. One, you need to grow your wealth perpetually. This means every week your wealth should be more than it was the week before, it doesn't need to be a lot more, but it needs to be more. Secondly, you need to grow your wealth exponentially. This is a powerful must that can help make up for a low income. By using compound interest growth strategies, over time you can win the wealth game. As you work through this program, you will clearly see how this works and why it is essential for building wealth. Unfortunately, those with the least are usually the least likely to use and benefit from this opportunity. This is unfortunate since it is available to anyone and so easy to use.

In the end, to be ultimately successful in life you will need to mate your wealth to your personal lifestyle in a way that allows true life balance and fulfillment. Often times financial success is handled carelessly and can unnecessarily have negative effects on your life. Regardless of how much money you have now or will build over time, this program will help show you what it takes to maintain balance and live a fulfilling life.

You **can** have the life of your dreams filled with the cars, homes, vacations, and all the other great luxuries life has to offer. Whatever your motivation, you can do it. But it has to start right here, right now, with you.

GET THIS

If you go no further in this program, at least do yourself a favor and be sure you get this one critical point! What you focus on is what you get. For better or worse, that's how life works—regardless of what you want. If your actions in life don't reflect that you understand how powerful this force is, you don't get it. Your subconscious mind will use **all** the inputs and information it has received from your conscious activities to establish your guiding principles. These principles affect your drive, mood, attitude, actions, and responses in everything you do.

So let me make becoming wealthy really easy for you. It's a one step process: just focus on it. Focus all of your conscious thoughts, mental inputs, and actions on becoming wealthy and you *will*. That may sound overly simple, but it's so true.

Your Conscious Focus

This is the intentional focus we put on something while we are awake and in control. When you are awake you get to steer the ship and direct what goes in to your mind. The things you focus on, have interest in, study, and surround yourself with are what will manifest in your life.

Your Inputs

You can't block out everything bad, nor live in a bubble. But you need to be a formidable gate keeper of what intel goes into your mind. There is a lot of stuff you don't want to consume in this world courtesy of the internet, cable television, games, and a million other sources of mind pollutants. You need to make a proactive effort to ensure that your mind is not getting filled with garbage that has no positive value to you. Worse yet, so much of what we consume daily can actually harm us and even kill any hope of fulfilling our dreams. So if you put in good, positive information, guess what? Your life will be positive and reflect what you put into it.

Your Subconscious Powerhouse

We focus the majority of our attention on our conscious thoughts and experiences with no regard for the most powerful and influential part of our mind. The subconscious mind steers our lives by building habits that influence our default actions based on the information it has previously received. These automatic responses will dictate our lives unless overridden by conscious choice and willpower—and we all know how well that typically works out.

The Take Away

To be a successful wealth builder you need to consciously, consistently, and proactively feed your mind information of only the most relevant and supportive types: the kinds that will lead you to naturally making superior decisions. You may say, "Ugh, I don't want to learn all this stuff!" I get that. But if you don't, you will struggle financially for a lifetime and *that* is ultimately much harder than figuring out wealth building.

Remember this key element. Most of the real learning and understanding of all the information you need to successfully build wealth happens subconsciously without any effort from you. So luckily, you don't have the full burden of trying to figure all of this out consciously.

NOTES:

_____
_____
_____
_____
_____
_____
_____
_____
_____
_____
_____
_____

FOUR KEYS TO BEING RICH

There are four keys that you must master to become and stay rich. All four are critical, and coming up short on just one can be the difference between making it and getting caught in a death spiral towards being emotionally and financially broke.

Behind each one of these benign-looking keys are a million different philosophies and strategies. What you will learn from this program is the Wealth Builder Lifestyle philosophy, which was created to make wealth building so simple and bulletproof that anyone can do it. By the end of this program you will fully understand how to use all of these keys without having to think about them. You will design a powerful Wealth Building Lifestyle that will be based on habitually creating wealth without the need for complex or cumbersome financial strategies.

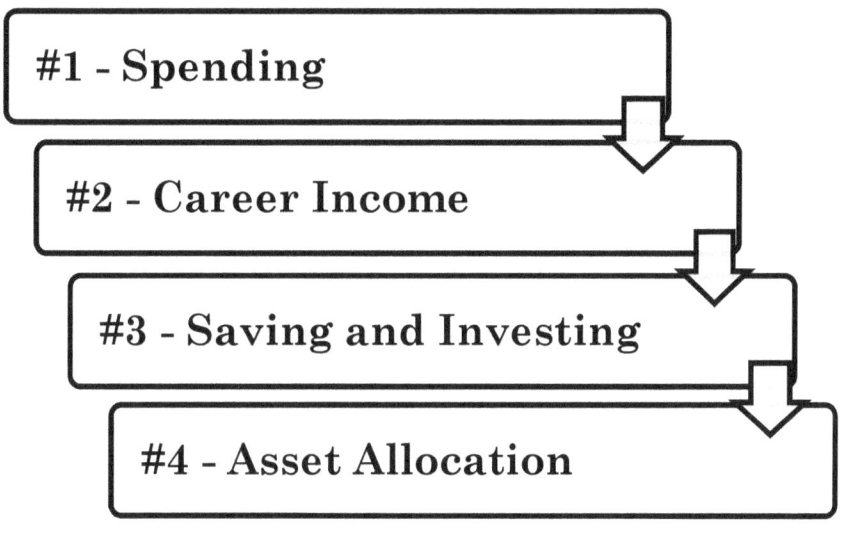

Spending

This is number one because regardless of how much you earn you can always outspend your income. How many people have you seen increase their income and then their spending right along with it? You could be earning $15,000 a month and still be living paycheck to paycheck.

It may seem obvious that you need to spend less than you earn, but many don't. There is an extreme amount of social pressure to have and do so many things that you can easily spend any amount of money.

THE REALITIES OF WEALTH TODAY

Career Income

Your career income is the fastest way for you to create wealth in your earlier years. A wealth builder needs to focus in on fast-tracking their careers early. Career fast-tracking is one of the largest topics covered in this program, and for good reason. The sooner we can get your career income up—even if only by a small percentage—the faster your wealth creation will grow and new doors of opportunity will open.

Saving and Investing

Anything you save is an investment in securing your future, regardless of whether it is earning a return or not. You will be establishing a personalized saving and investing plan based specifically on your income and financial situation. It will be designed with the sole intent of catapulting you into the strongest possible wealth building scenario. Your investment income will eventually subsidize or replace your career income as your career income fades or ends all together.

Asset Allocation

Last but not least by any means is asset allocation. Regardless of how much wealth you have built it needs to be kept safe from any one market fluctuation. Ask all those people that lost their homes during the "housing crisis" how important asset allocation is. So many people had all their past wealth and current income going into their home only to have it swept out from under their feet due to a market shift. Unfortunately, since they weren't properly prepared, there was little they could do to prevent it.

Being Rich Is Not Being Wealthy

No amount of money will ever lead to lasting happiness. Let's face it: you don't want to be rich so you can have a bunch of pieces of paper with dead presidents on them. I know plenty of people that are definitively rich but no happier than some of my poor acquaintances—maybe even less so.

If you are following this program solely with the intent of getting financially rich, you may find the money more of a curse than a blessing. Unless you understand what it really takes to have a fulfilling life, money will only help you live a similar life to what you currently have in a more opulent style. Make no mistake, if your heart and intentions are in pursuit of money for the wrong reasons, you can expect lots of pain to accompany your success.

Which brings me to my next point. There may be four keys to being rich, but there is..

ONLY ONE WAY TO BE WEALTHY

If you truly want to be wealthy in your life, you need to look outside of money and into successfully living a fulfilling life. This is an extensive topic on its own so there is no way it's going to fit in this book, but I do want to share the broad concept with you. If you will keep these seven human needs in mind as you go through this course and life in general, all aspects of your life will make more sense and you will have much greater control over your happiness.

The Seven Human Needs

The human needs aspect of this program is designed to help you understand what motivates all humans. These needs are not something we can just put off meeting—they *have* to be successfully met to live any kind of meaningful life. A great life can never be achieved without substantially meeting most or all of these needs. Understanding these needs and keeping them well served in all aspects of your life will give you the opportunity to live a truly enjoyable and fulfilling life.

The needs below are listed in the order of significance in our lives. This does not mean that we all value and work to meet these needs in this particular order.

Sustenance

This is the essential need we all must meet to even *exist*. We meet this requirement with things like food, water, shelter, money, and other items we would perish without.

Connection

Connection is the most powerful and influential need we all have, and often one of the most underserved and overlooked. Without question, this is an area you want to focus a lot of attention on. If you are ever in a pinch and need someone to lean on or help you find an opportunity, the most reliable source for a solution is in your connections. Even a loose connection can often provide some wisdom or make you aware of an opportunity that can resolve your problem.

Our need for connection must be met from many meaningful sources including family, friends, strangers, coworkers, pets, the environment, and society in general. When you have the capability to make significant connections on a deeper level, an entire new world of opportunity and security will open up to you.

THE REALITIES OF WEALTH TODAY

Security

Frequently the most focused on need, security, gives us the certainty that we can do things like take care of our family. We will often forgo our connection need to instead dedicate our focus and energy towards meeting our security need. This makes sense at first glance, but in reality the easiest way to meet and achieve security is to have and maintain solid connections.

Growth

To live a fulfilling life you *need* to constantly be growing. There are no plateaus that allow for you to remain in one spot. Life is constantly in motion, moving in one direction or another, and by choosing to grow you avoid contracting. Growing your education, finances, experiences, and so on keeps life interesting and provides a feeling of truly being alive.

Significance

We all need to feel significant, like we matter. This feeling adds meaning to our lives, builds us up, and makes us feel important. Often times this need is very ego driven: why do we want to build an empire, have fancy cars, and own nice things? It's because in today's society those things are symbols of success—meaning you have achieved something beyond average—and are therefore special.

We need to be very careful when serving this need because it is too easily met in unhealthy, immoral, or selfish ways. Those negative approaches defy our inner human values and will never provide anything other than short-term results.

Esteem

When this need is fulfilled, it's often because we are achieving things. We have the respect of others, feel confident, are proud, and are experiencing increased drive. Esteem is not to be mistaken for just self-esteem, they are both equally important. Our need is met in two ways: internally, through self-esteem (how we truly think and feel about ourselves), and externally, through esteem (which is how we are regarded and seen by others).

As anyone knows, having self-esteem is a very important aspect of being successful. Less focused on in today's "me" society, however, is the power of regular esteem. Today, we are more likely to bully or buy our way through or around obstacles. This may work out in the short-term, but it's not a lasting approach.

ONLY ONE WAY TO BE WEALTHY

Inner Peace

Inner peace is what compels us to continually pursue all of our other needs. Should we fail to successfully fulfill them in healthy ways that align with our values, we will feel pain. The further away we are from satisfying our needs, the more pain and despair we can expect.

The key to meeting this seventh need is first focusing on meeting the other six. Once you have mastered that, you will have energy, passion, and drive like never before. This will bring you to the final step, which is acceptance. When you accept your life and its purpose you can then feel at peace and ultimately fulfilled. Unchecked, our quest for inner peace will either drive us to success (if we're lucky) or insanity (if careless). Nonetheless, we will continue our pursuit until we achieve it or reach our end. This may all seem like psycho babble, but I assure you it's not. It's undeniable that every human has the need to meet these seven elements. Take a look at anyone who is truly successful financially, career-wise, in relationships, in regard to life balance, in parenting, and in all the other aspects of their lives. You will find that they will all have these two things in common:

1. They will be substantially meeting most (if not all) of their needs.
2. They will be very influential in helping others meet their own needs.

That being said, few successful people would actually be able to tell you about their human needs or how they meet them. They don't need to because they have picked up habits that effectively meet their needs throughout their upbringing and life experiences. In a way, you could say they're just lucky. But success does not require you to be lucky. Once exposed to and made aware of these needs, anyone can reshape the environments and habits of their life to adequately meet them. The beauty is that when you are meeting your needs, you will realize just how little money it actually takes to live a rich and fulfilling life.

Balancing Self and Public Image

One of the most powerful forces that can work against wealth building (especially in the U.S.) is maintaining an image of wealth. The reason why said image can get the better of so many is due to the fact that it artificially meets some of the seven human needs. This is no joke. This *will* be an Achilles heel for many aspiring wealth builders.

Unfortunately, if you are putting off wealth building and spending money to support an image you can't afford, some day you will be delivered a harsh and unforgiving reality. The following are some brief examples of how spending can meet some needs and support your image unnaturally.

THE REALITIES OF WEALTH TODAY

Sustenance

Having income or cash flow can easily satisfy this need, especially if you are not consciously aware of your overall financial picture and risk. Being a little low on money may not trigger concern when another paycheck is expected soon.

Connection

By using money, you can be the life of the party. Thanks to your artificially rich image, you can have an abundance of social interactions and a long list of people waiting to hang out with you. With all those connections and great times, your friends and family will rally around you and worship you like a god—at least until the money is gone.

Security

Once again, without a clear understanding of your finances and the world of money, you can foolishly believe you are secure just because you have another paycheck due in the near future. As naïve as that is, this can falsely appear to meet your security need.

Growth

Taking trips, seeing places, figuring out how to operate the new smart TV, growing your credit lines, meeting new people, and so on are all sources of growth that will meet this need right up until you run out of money. This may project an image of having a great life while in reality you're living on the edge.

Significance

Spending is the number one socially accepted method for attempting to artificially meet our need for significance. Drive a fancy car, wear fancy clothes, or own all the latest gadgets and toys and you will feel and look very significant indeed.

Esteem

When you have an abundance of friends and your needs are met (even artificially), you are going to feel pretty good about yourself and how you are viewed by others.

Inner Peace

You may have moments of bliss, but if you have any kind of financial intelligence—even just a little bit—you are going to have some concern about the what-ifs. What if my income stops? How long can I sustain myself if that happens? Questions like these won't have good long-term answers. Unfortunately, many will just accept their needs being artificially met and continue enjoying the moments of bliss in the present without any regard for the future fallout.

You do not want your worth tied to money that someday you may not be able to obtain or that you find may be in limited supply. When people that live that way suffer from financial setbacks, a huge void forms on their "needs being met" list and they feel distraught. Others have even taken their own lives just to get out of the pain of feeling so empty and broken. That is not a game that's worth playing, especially when there are better options.

Four States of Living

Regardless of the amount of wealth you have or want, you need to be conscious of the state you are living in. Make sure the state you are spending most of your time in is serving the ultimate goal of living a fulfilling life.

Intentionally sacrificing for a period of time can greatly accelerate growth, which may (for some) be the shortest path to a life of fulfillment. That being said, we need to make every effort to ensure that we do not get stuck in a lifestyle of sacrificing and/or sustaining. This happens all too often since these take the least amount of effort and require very little proactive action to attain.

This graphic illustrates the states we ideally want to spend the most time living our lives in.

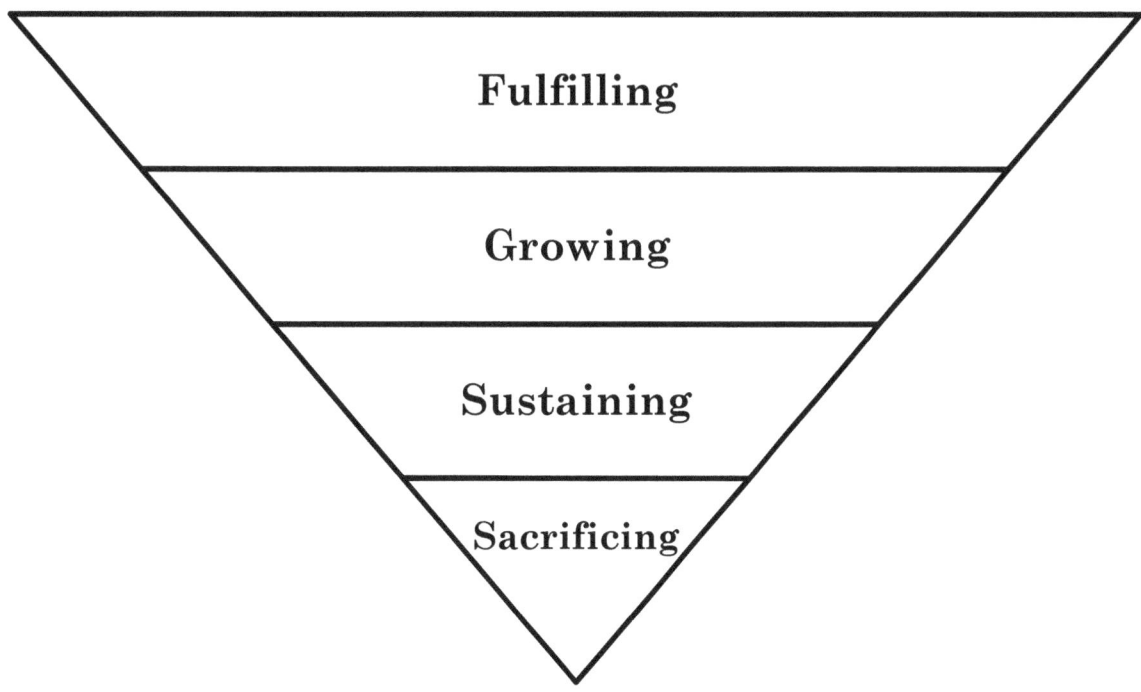

THE REALITIES OF WEALTH TODAY

Sacrificing

Sacrificing is not a state we want to live our lives in forever. On the other hand, short stays with the intent of leveraging an opportunity that has long-term benefits which can propel us up into a better state of living can often make sense.

Sustaining

This can be one of the most limiting and dangerous states of living. Often times when people are able to sustain themselves, they tend to fall into the old cliché of "this is making a living." Without intention or awareness of the importance of building real wealth, this can become a trap that can lead to spending the last years of your life in a forced state of sacrificing.

Growing

Growing can be one of the most fulfilling states of living, but it typically requires clear goals and decisive intentions to enter into and maintain this state. A lifestyle involving growth will open doors to many of life's greatest opportunities.

Fulfillment

A life in balance (filled with growth and the rewards of achievement in many areas of life) can lead to the greatest state of living, and ultimately, a life of fulfillment.

NOTES :

_____
_____
_____
_____
_____
_____
_____
_____
_____
_____

LIFE CYCLES
AFFECT AND INFLUENCE EVERYTHING

Life cycles are essentially the changing states that everything goes through. Depending on the life cycle stage something is in, it will often return different results or responses. Some of these life cycles are well known and focused on, especially in business. Not taking these into consideration in business can lead to large profit losses or worse—going out of business.

These life cycles are also present in our daily lives. They affect our income potential, household expenses, transportation costs, personal expenditures, education, and on and on. Although life cycles affect everyone, it depends on the individual's situation when and how they will show effect.

Putting off investing until your income is substantial enough to contribute larger amounts is foolish. Even small amounts invested early on will turn into large sums by the time you retire. So don't underestimate the power of the compound interest life cycle.

NOTES :

_____
_____
_____
_____
_____
_____
_____
_____
_____
_____
_____
_____

THE REALITIES OF WEALTH TODAY
Career Income Life Cycle

A good example of an important life cycle involves our income-earning potential.

Stage One encompasses ages 18-25 when we have few skills, low income, and less stability.

Stage Two encompasses ages 25-35 when we have high skill development, increasing income, and more stability.

Stage Three encompasses ages 35-50 when we are in our peak-earning years. We are masters of our skills, have the highest income-earning potential, and are very stable.

Stage Four encompasses ages 50-65, which I call the twilight years of earning. We are coming off of our peak: our skills are fading, our income has likely stagnated (or may be decreasing), and our job stability is in question. Losing a job at this stage in life can mean a huge pay reduction and possibly even permanent unemployment.

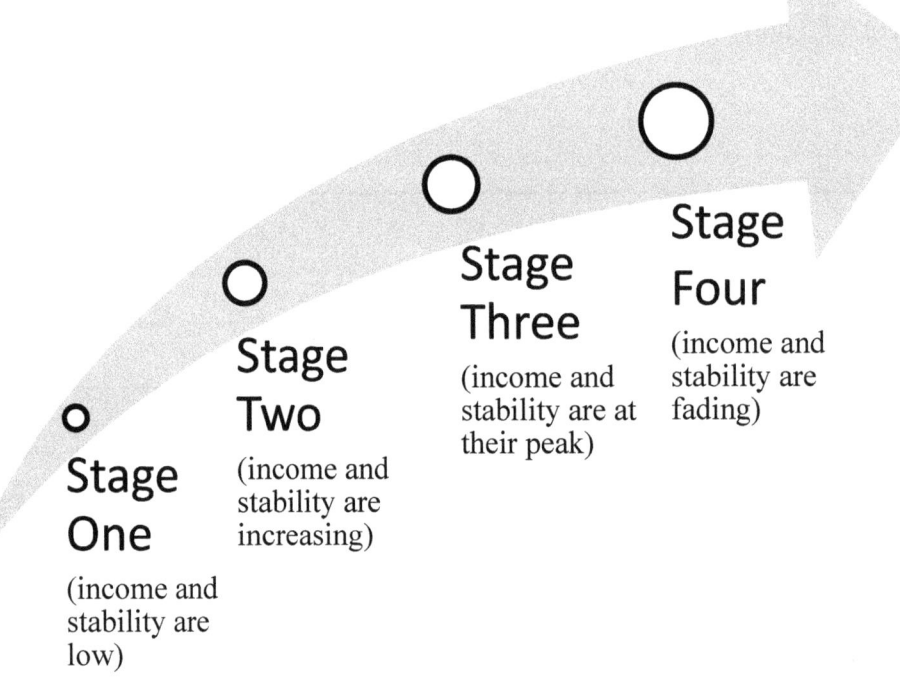

"Expecting to be wealthy without a clear picture of what it takes for you to be wealthy and a clear plan to get you there will keep you right where you are."
- Daniel Hartjoy

LIFE CYCLES AFFECT AND INFLUENCE EVERYTHING

Investment Income Life Cycle

Now, with the career income life cycle in mind, look at the investment income life cycle and see how they can work with or against each other. The most powerful time to invest is when your income is in Stage One because even a small investment at this point will be exploding in value during Stage Four of your career income-earning cycle (which, if you'll recall, is when stability and income potential are falling). A lifetime of good investing habits can lead to eventually replacing your lost career income with investment income. Unfortunately, most will wait until they have an abundance of extra money to start investing, resulting in their investments not having the necessary time to reach their own peak growth cycles.

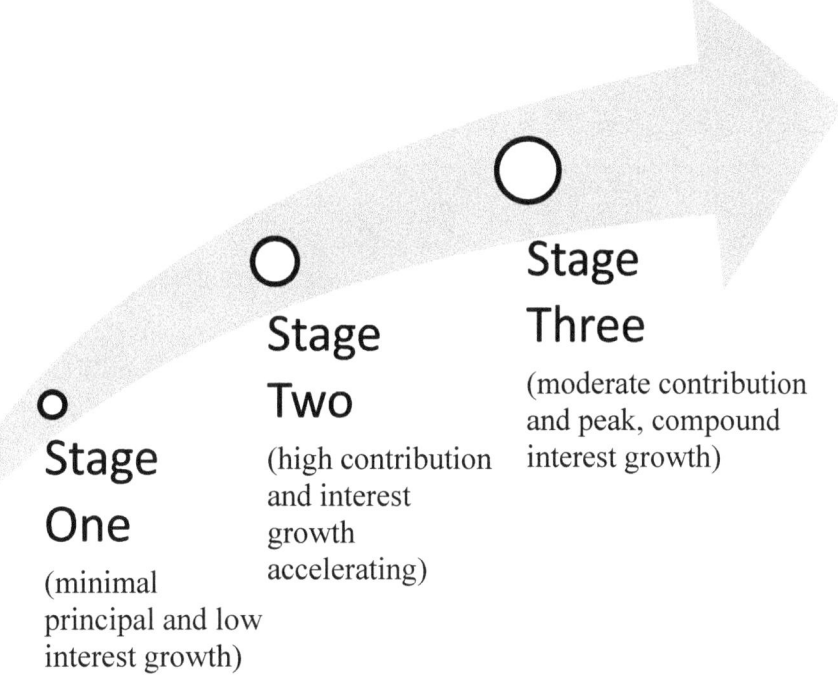

Stage One (minimal principal and low interest growth)

Stage Two (high contribution and interest growth accelerating)

Stage Three (moderate contribution and peak, compound interest growth)

For you to successfully control and leverage lifecycles to their fullest benefit requires a broad analysis. To successfully capitalize on them you often times have to work the yin against the yang (and vice versa). So a narrow focus on one problem (the yin, or the career income in this case) may keep you from seeing the natural solution that comes from the yang (the future investment income).

When it comes to wealth building, career and investment incomes should be viewed as one interconnected tool. The optimal way to build wealth is through a balanced two-prong approach. When you retire and your paycheck stops, your investments will continue to produce income through the end of your days.

THE VALUE OF A DOLLAR

We hear about the dollar losing value all the time these days. For some this may be the case, but for the people living the Wealth Builder Lifestyle it's actually far from it. By having their money invested into an investment that is earning a compound return that *exceeds* the rate of inflation, their dollars are not losing but instead *gaining* value.

The next time you spend a dollar on something you could do without, consider what that dollar would be worth if you stashed it away in an investment instead. The following chart illustrates just that—the explosive returns you could expect from compound interest. Teaching your kids to put away even small amounts of money when they are young will allow them to easily build wealth throughout their own lifetime (and retire with financial security).

The saying "time is money" is absolutely true when it comes to investing. A $1 investment with a 10% return will grow to $7.32 in 20 years. That's not bad, seeing as that's over seven times its original value. But let it compound *another* 20 years and it will be worth a whopping $53.70! That's over 53 times the value.

This chart shows what an investment of just $1 (one time) would be worth over different periods of time based on varying rates of return.

Value Over Time of $1 Investment (Excluding tax consequences)						
Return	1 Year	5 Years	10 Years	20 Years	30 Years	40 Years
3.0%	$1.03	$1.16	$1.34	$1.82	$2.45	$3.31
5.0%	$1.05	$1.28	$1.64	$2.71	$4.46	$7.35
7.5%	$1.07	$1.45	$2.11	$4.46	$9.42	$19.89
10.0%	$1.10	$1.64	$2.70	$7.32	$19.83	$53.70
12.5%	$1.13	$1.86	$3.46	$12.02	$41.70	$144.62
15.0%	$1.16	$2.10	$4.44	$19.71	$87.54	$388.70
17.5%	$1.18	$2.38	$5.68	$32.28	$183.47	$1,042.57
20.0%	$1.21	$2.69	$7.26	$62.84	$383.96	$2,790.74
22.5%	$1.24	$3.04	$9.29	$86.34	$802.31	$7,455.18
25.0%	$1.28	$3.44	$11.87	$140.98	$1,673.95	$19,875.79

This also illustrates the harsh reality of waiting to start investing. The peak return on long-term, compound interest investments comes in the later years, so the longer it has to work the more it can do. Consider this: to be a millionaire after 40 years, you only need to invest $18,621 one time into a 10% return investment. And if you could pull off a 15% return, that amount drops to just $2,572.

Debt Reduction Investing

If you want to swing quickly from financial fool to fast-track wealth builder, here is one way to do it. Say you're just getting started, but are amped up and ready to take a small step. You have decided that you can immediately put $50 a month into your new Wealth Builder Lifestyle. If you have any short-term debt, one of the best investments you can make is getting yourself out of it.

I'm going to assume for this example that you have some credit card debt (as the majority of people do). Let's say you owe $5,000 worth, and let's also assume the interest rate on that debt is 18%. Now, I'm sure *you* don't have that debt, but maybe a friend does so stay tuned. Maybe this bit of insight could be shared and do them some good.

I'm going to illustrate this in a few different ways so you can understand the deeper dynamics in play. These are all things that banks and wealthy people know and habitually avoid. One of the keys to this wealth building system is to get you into good habits and away from the bad ones. Regardless of whether you fully understand the reasoning, this will help you minimize wealth loss and be more likely to create it.

First, let's look at your debt based on the previously outlined criteria. Assuming you will pay it off using the minimum payment (calculated by the lender at 2% of the balance), here are the numbers:

Typical Payoff

Initial Debt: **$5,000**

Initial Payment: **$100**

Total Interest Paid (wealth squandered): **$11,898**

Time to Pay Off: **32 years and 10 months**

Look at the dramatic difference in this next example that would result if you made just one extra payment of $50 towards this card (and then paid it off using the minimum payment schedule):

THE VALUE OF A DOLLAR

One $50 Extra Payment
(then typical payoff)

Initial Debt: **$5,000**

Initial Payment: **$100**

One-Time Payment: **$50**

Total Interest Paid (wealth squandered): **$11,348**

Time to Pay Off: **31 years and 8 months**

That $50 actually saves you $500 over the life of the loan and shortens the loan by 1 year and 2 months! Now, let's say you lock yourself into a new, self-imposed minimum payment of $150 (which is essentially your current minimum payment plus a $50 investment). This is what it would look like doing some debt investing in yourself:

Fixed Payment Debt Investing

Initial Debt: **$5,000**

New Debt-Investment Payment: **$150**

Total Interest Paid (wealth squandered): **$1,835**

Time to Pay Off: **3 years and 10 months**

That debt-investment wealth building strategy will save you a whopping $10,063 in less than four years! If you don't have that extra money already, then you really need to ask yourself how you can afford to give away over $10,000 to a bank.

Before we go any further, here's a tip: **never just pay the minimum payment!** Never, never, never. So, you don't have enough money to pay any more? Fine! Take a pass for this month. But next month when your bill comes (and every following month until it is paid off), pay at least what you paid this month.

I would estimate that two years after someone makes $5,000 worth of credit card charges, their retained value is no more than $1,000. If anything that was purchased is still around, the total value you would likely receive by selling them off would be less than $1,000. So that $5,000 you still owe is now offset by only $1,000 in assets, leaving your net worth down by a loss of $4,000. Had you held off on buying whatever you had to have and just contributed that money to a growth equity fund that managed a 10% return (which is still very possible in this market) your picture would have looked a lot different.

THE REALITIES OF WEALTH TODAY

To see just how dramatically different, look at the following two examples:

Fixed Payment Credit Card Payoff

Credit Card Expenditures: **$5,000**

Fixed Monthly Payment: **$100**

Total of Payments (Principal and Interest): **$9,019**

Indebted Period: **7 years and 7 months**

End Value of Items Purchased (if anything): **Less Than $1,000**

That's right, the total residual value of your $9,019 investment likely turns out to be less than $1,000.

Investing Debt Payment Equivalent
(investment at a 10% return)

Fixed Monthly Contribution: **$100**

Total of Investment: **$9,019**

Payment Period: **7 years and 7 months**

End Value of Investment: **$13,649**

The amount of free money earned just for making good decisions? A whopping $4,630. Now, here's the amazing part: the net wealth difference between the first example (the average American) and the second one (a wealth builder) is $12,649 in the wealth builder's favor. The sad part is that the average person will not likely pay off their debt in the 7 years and 7 months but rather ride repayment out for far longer (or in the worst case until they file bankruptcy).

"Take strategic actions to create exceptional results with minimal effort!"
- Daniel Hartjoy

THE VALUE OF A DOLLAR
Educate Kids Early About Money

If you have children (or are planning on having children), you have a moral obligation to pass on good wealth building habits to the next generation. The poorer your habits are the more important it is for you to break the cycle. In the past you may have had an excuse like, "I didn't know, so it's not my fault," but that got tossed out the window when you put your hands on The Wealth Builder Lifestyle.

Towards the end of this book is a section dedicated specifically to passing on the habits of a Wealth Builder Lifestyle to your children. Once you begin sharing this information with them, you will be amazed at how quickly they pick it up and the depths at which they understand it. Make it a point to share all the details about what we cover in this book. It can open up some great conversations and give them a head start on learning what they need to know about money to become successful.

Teach basic investing *now*. When the balance in a savings account reaches $1,000, show them how to open a custodial investment account. A good initial investment is a growth and income mutual fund. Teens can go online and research the performance and ratings to help choose their own investments.

Teach them early on about building their retirement. Waiting until that first full-time job to learn about investments and 401(k) plans is a mistake. The sooner they start saving for retirement, the more likely they will pick up good financial habits and reap the benefits of compound interest.

NOTES :

___
___
___
___
___
___
___
___

PART ONE:
CURRENT WEALTH STATUS

FINANCIAL STATUS TEST

Take a few minutes to go through this Financial Status Test. It will help you quickly analyze your situation to get an idea of your current financial lifestyle. Are you currently living as a super-charged wealth builder, or as a master of wealth destruction? This test is designed to get a pulse on how you are doing in twenty key aspects of a financially successful lifestyle.

Date: ____/____/_____

Next to each section mark down a rating from 1 to 10 where 10 equates to being perfect (with no room or desire for improvement), 5 is satisfactory—not bad, but not great—and 1 equates to being in serious need of improvement.

_____	1) **Financial Security** – How close are you to having at least three months of expenses available in cash or liquid assets?	_____	2) **Disability and Life Insurance** – Are you financially ready in the event of a surprise (such as a disability or death)?
_____	3) **Assets** – Do you currently have an asset growth plan in place? Are you consistently increasing your assets?	_____	4) **Spending** – Is your current spending lifestyle in balance? Are you currently living within your means?
_____	5) **Budget** – Do you currently have (and follow) a budget? Does your lifestyle reflect financial discipline and a long-term plan?	_____	6) **Short-Term Debt** – Is your credit card, auto, and other short-term debt minimal? Do you limit your credit card use?
_____	7) **Debt Elimination** – Are you currently debt free or working on a debt reduction plan? Is your debt trending downward?	_____	8) **Career (Excluding Pay)** – Rate the fulfillment and enjoyment you get from your career and work environment.
_____	9) **Income** – Is your income ideal? Put the number that represents the financial percentile of where you feel you are (i.e. seven for 70%). Approximating is fine!	_____	10) **Security Investments** – Are you currently saving a percentage of your income in cash or secure investments (such as precious metals or your home)?
_____	11) **Growth Investments** – Do you have a strategy in place to consistently grow a portfolio of growth investments?	_____	12) **Business Investments** – Do you have a high-growth investment strategy that will get you where you want to go?
_____	13) **Net Worth** – Do you frequently track your net worth (what you own minus what you owe)? (10 - monthly, 1 - never)	_____	14) **Environment** – Does your environment offer the career and lifestyle opportunities necessary to reach your goals?
_____	15) **Associations** – Are you surrounded with friends and colleagues that are supportive lifestyle role models?	_____	16) **Knowledge** – Do you actively continue to grow your knowledge in your career, financial skills, and other aspects of life?
_____	17) **Esteem** – Are you proud of your current career and financial status? Do you feel you are doing the best you can?	_____	18) **Contribution** – Do you show gratitude for your successes by contributing back to others and society?
_____	19) **Dream Lifestyle** – Are you currently financially capable of living your dream lifestyle while still building wealth?	_____	20) **Fulfillment** – Is everything in your life adding up? Do you feel you are getting what you want out of life?

PART ONE: CURRENT WEALTH STATUS

Scoring the Test

1. Add up all the individual scores you entered and write down your grand total.
2. Divide your grand total by two and then enter that number below as your score.

Grand Total _____   Your Score_____%

Change Your Status

So, how did you score? Maybe you are less than thrilled, and that's ok. It actually makes sense when you think about it. You internally knew you could be doing better—that's the whole reason why you picked up this program. The great news is that you've already made it this far, which says you are someone who will actually take the new actions necessary to improve your life. And you and I both know that change requires different actions. Look at anyone that is stuck and you will see that they continue to do the same things over and over (thus getting the same results). Even a small action that creates a little change has the potential to cause a ripple effect that can eventually lead to a major difference in outcome.

This is known as the "butterfly effect," which is really an amazing theory. If you have never heard of it or don't fully understand how it works, do a little research on the topic. Heck, there's even a movie called the *Butterfly Effect* with Ashton Kutcher in it that actually provides a great illustration of how even a minor change can affect the trajectory of your life in major ways you never thought possible.

On the following page take your three lowest scores and write the aspects to improve. These are the areas that you have the most room to improve in. Bringing these up just a few points will significantly improve your life. Write down some actions you can immediately take that will create significant changes in the areas you need to improve the most.

NOTES :

_____

_____

_____

_____

_____

FINANCIAL STATUS TEST
Three Major Target Areas to Improve:

1. Opportunity for Improvement: _____
   I will immediately take the following actions to improve this aspect of my life:

   _____

   _____

   _____

2. Opportunity for Improvement: _____
   I will immediately take the following actions to improve this aspect of my life:

   _____

   _____

   _____

3. Opportunity for Improvement: _____
   I will immediately take the following actions to improve this aspect of my life:

   _____

   _____

   _____

Let's face it: money is a manmade essential need for modern life. In our contemporary world, not much happens without some kind of financial persuasion behind it. Managing money can be relatively easy, but there are still many forces working nonstop to reduce its value (and many more trying to find a way to get those dollars from you).

We are going to begin by creating a snapshot of your current financial picture. Just follow the steps on the next page and fill in the worksheets to see exactly where you are. Most people are absolutely amazed when they get a clear picture of their current financial situation. For some, it's a good surprise and for others, it's a serious wake up call.

"You can't save your way to prosperity, but you can spend your way to poverty!"
- Daniel Hartjoy

SPENDING

Although you can't just save your way to prosperity, being aware of your spending habits and refocusing some of your discretionary spending can greatly accelerate your wealth creation. Investing the value of just one $3 cup of coffee a day at a 10% return for the next 30 years would turn into $187,188. That means your total investment of $32,400, will have generated $154,788 in free wealth.

For the next 24 hours, challenge yourself to write down all of your discretionary expenses. Seriously! Don't just think about it. Carry a notepad in your pocket to note the item and cost of each of your purchases. At the end of the 24 hours, add up the total. Did it turn out to be more or less than you would have guessed?

You may not currently have all the information to fill out every category in this next form, but that's ok. Things like health, disability, and life insurance will be discussed in further detail on the following pages. Any items not captured in one of the specific lines should be entered into the "Other" row of the corresponding category.

NOTES :

_____
_____
_____
_____
_____
_____
_____
_____
_____
_____
_____

PART ONE: CURRENT WEALTH STATUS

Work through the following calculations to establish your monthly minimum expenses.

Current Spending Expenses			
Housing Expenses		**Personal Expenses**	
Rent or mortgage	$ _____	Clothes	$ _____
Real Property Taxes	$ _____	Education	$ _____
Home/Renters Insurance	$ _____	Other Personal	$ _____
Maintenance and Repairs	$ _____	**Total Personal Expenses**	$ _____
Other Housing	$ _____	**Fun Money Expenses**	
Total Housing	$ _____	Entertainment	$ _____
Necessity Expenses		Travel and Gifts	$ _____
Utilities (All combined)	$ _____	Other Fun Stuff	$ _____
Health Insurance	$ _____	**Total Fun Money**	$ _____
Disability Insurance	$ _____	**Short-Term Debt Expenses**	
Term Life Insurance	$ _____	Short-Term Debt	$ _____
Phones, Cable, Internet	$ _____	**Total Short-Term Debt**	$ _____
Groceries and Household	$ _____		
Auto (all related expenses)	$ _____		
Laundry	$ _____	**Total Monthly Spending**	$ _____
Other Necessity	$ _____		
Total Necessity	$ _____		

Did you find any surprises in your spending habits? Sometimes just grouping and listing the items out can shed some light on potential areas of overspending. Often times we discover "sleeper" categories, or rather categories that we didn't realize we spend so much in. Sometimes just the discovery of these areas can get us motivated enough to make changes that can free up some money to apply towards a better use.

INCOME

Enter your monthly income information in the following form. If you only have the annual number, just divide it by twelve and input that amount. Our primary goal is to determine your net monthly income, so if you don't have your gross income numbers don't worry about it. Having them available can, however, be enlightening.

One of the not-so-secret secrets of the rich are tax shelters. These are used to reduce the amount of taxes that are paid on your gross income. This can in turn increase your net income or take-home pay without increasing your gross income. Essentially, this gives you a higher income without you having to actually earn more.

Current Monthly Income		
Income Source	Gross Income (before taxes)	Net Income (after taxes)
Wages and Tips	$_____	$_____
Long-Term Investments	$_____	$_____
High-Growth Investments	$_____	$_____
Business Investments	$_____	$_____
Property Investments	$_____	$_____
Refunds/Re-imbursements	$_____	$_____
Other Income	$_____	$_____
Total Income (all sources)	$_____	$_____

One sad fact of the financially undereducated is that they think raising taxes on the rich will somehow benefit them. The financially wise use tax shelters and loopholes to avoid paying these higher taxes, and any taxes they do have to pay will ultimately be passed on to employees through lower pay, reduced benefits, or (in the worst case) staff reductions. It's not an evil conspiracy, there's just no other way to pay for it. This is why the lowest-income earners always suffer from higher taxes. Either directly or indirectly, **the poorest people have always carried the tax burden,** regardless of which nation they call home. The solution is not more taxes, it's learning how to build wealth.

DEBT

As I demonstrated earlier, short-term debt is the archenemy of wealth building. This easy-to-obtain debt is like a virus and hard for many to shake. In most cases, short-term debt eats away at wealth faster than most wealth building techniques can create it, especially when compared dollar-for-dollar.

One of the best ways to jumpstart your wealth building plan is by paying off high-interest, short-term debt. Think about this: to break even with the financial losses created by $5,000 worth of credit card debt at an APR of 20%, you would need to have over $10,000 invested and earning a 10% annual return. The investment amount has to be so high because not only does it have to cover the amount lost to credit card debt interest, but also the income taxes (the ones I just spoke about) on your investment.

NOTES :

_____
_____
_____
_____
_____
_____
_____
_____
_____
_____
_____
_____

PART ONE: CURRENT WEALTH STATUS

Use the next form to start forming a short-term debt-payoff plan. Start by entering your creditors, loan balances, and interest rates right off your last statements. Then comes the tricky part. Use a calculator to complete the following two formulas and fill in the last two columns.

Short-Term Debts

Monthly Interest - Loan Balance × Interest Rate ÷ 12 = Monthly Interest
Example loan: $3,500 × 0.16 = $560 ÷ 12 = $46.67 (0.16 equals 16 percent)
Monthly Principal - Minimum Payment – Monthly Interest = Monthly Principal
Example loan: $60.00 - $46.67 = $13.33

Current Short-Term Debts					
Creditor	Loan Balance	Interest Rate	Minimum Payment	Monthly Interest	Monthly Principal
Example Loan	*$3,500*	*16%*	*$60*	*$46.67*	*$13.33*
_____	$_____	___%	$_____	$_____	$_____
_____	$_____	___%	$_____	$_____	$_____
_____	$_____	___%	$_____	$_____	$_____
_____	$_____	___%	$_____	$_____	$_____
_____	$_____	___%	$_____	$_____	$_____
_____	$_____	___%	$_____	$_____	$_____
_____	$_____	___%	$_____	$_____	$_____
_____	$_____	___%	$_____	$_____	$_____
Combined Totals	$_____		$_____	$_____	$_____

If you need more space, make copies of this page as needed. Enter the combined total of all the columns (excluding the interest rate one). You'll be using this information later when creating your unique Rebalance Blueprint.

NOTES :

_____
_____
_____

SAVINGS AND INVESTMENTS

It's no wonder so many people in the United States are struggling financially. Without a good saving and investing plan, we dramatically limit our wealth-creation potential. Most people don't have the income and discipline necessary to save adequately for the future. A good saving and investment plan can help make up for any shortcomings in earning potential.

Let's take a look at your current investing habits. The point of investing is not about creating a better financial situation today. (That being said, every time you invest yours will be improving). It's really about planting the seeds that will eventually generate the wealth you will need down the road.

In the following form, enter the amount you currently contribute to savings and investments. The following category descriptions will help you determine what type of investments you are presently making based on the Wealth Builder Lifestyle philosophy.

Security Investments

These are cash, precious metals, or other reasonably safe investments like your home, safer growth mutual funds, Certificates of Deposit, and other low-risk investments. These should be very safe with an annual return goal of approximately 7%.

Growth Investments

These are higher-return investments that are used to accelerate your wealth building which may be less liquid and have higher potential risk. They may include things like growth and income (as well as international) mutual funds (which can be reasonably safe investments that have potential for returns of 10% or higher).

Business Investments

These funds are used for your own personal business, investments directly into other companies, or things like more aggressive mutual funds. These will likely be higher-risk and have potential annual returns in excess of 15%.

PART ONE: CURRENT WEALTH STATUS

Work through the following saving and investing habits form.

Current Savings and Investments			
Category	Combined Net Monthly Income	Average Monthly Contribution	Monthly Percentage Invested (contribution ÷ income)
Example Category	*$2,540*	*$150*	*6%*
Security Investments		$ _____	_____%
Growth Investments	$ _____	$ _____	_____%
Business Investments		$ _____	_____%
Combined Savings and Investments		$ _____	_____%

Do you currently feel you have an adequate investment strategy to prepare you for retirement and to cover you in the event of any unplanned setback? Yes ___ No ___

If not, what areas do you feel could use some improvement?

_____
_____

How would you feel if (by taking the actions in this program) you were able to eliminate all of those areas of concern?

_____
_____

How would your life be different, and what would it look like?

_____
_____

Saving and investing is not easy for most. As our financial education grows, so can our wealth. If you don't already invest, start now, not some day when you get around to it! Life moves too fast to take a chance on waiting.

FINANCIAL SECURITY CUSHION

Someday, it's going to rain. Don't get caught off guard. What I mean is, rarely do people have enough liquid wealth set aside to cover an unanticipated loss of income or other financial setback. This often leads to a rapid and excessive loss of wealth, damaged credit, or even bankruptcy. Everyone should have a plan to deal with an income interruption (preferably adequate enough to cover at least six months) using only cash and liquid assets.

A liquid asset is an asset that can be immediately converted into cash without substantial penalties. A non-liquid (or fixed) asset would be something like real estate, a car, a boat, or any other item that would take some time to convert to cash. Things like an IRA or 401K are not necessarily good liquid assets. Although you may be able to convert them into cash quickly, the taxes and penalties will only add to your financial setback.

NOTES :

_____
_____
_____
_____
_____
_____
_____
_____
_____
_____
_____
_____

PART ONE: CURRENT WEALTH STATUS

Before we move away from your current financial picture, perform the following calculations to determine how many months you could last without part or all of your current income. If you are in a dual-income household, evaluate the possible loss of one or both incomes.

Current Financial Security Cushion		
Option	**Amount**	**Calculation**
Example Cash & Liquid Assets $<u>7,500.00</u> ÷	$2,500.00 - $5,000.00 = -$2,500.00 =	← New Income ← Minimum Monthly Expenses __3__ Months Without Income
Variation One Cash and Liquid Assets $_____ ÷	$_____ - $_____ = $_____ =	← New Income ← Minimum Monthly Expenses _____ Months Without Income
Variation Two Cash and Liquid Assets $_____ ÷	$_____ - $_____ = $_____ =	← New Income ← Minimum Monthly Expenses _____ Months Without Income

Regardless of your current situation, as you work through your custom plan we will make sure that you are building up an adequate security cushion. These things will not happen overnight, which is why I say that building wealth is a lifestyle and not just an event.

NOTES :

_____
_____
_____
_____
_____

CURRENT NET WORTH

If you truly want to achieve a goal, you need to have a way to monitor and measure your progress. Everyone should know and continually monitor their net worth. Some financial gurus will advise you to primarily focus on your income and cash flow. I'm very fond of an approach that includes those aspects, but not in lieu of building your net worth and a diversified asset base.

If you're new to tracking your wealth (or are starting with little to no wealth/net worth), I would advise you to track your net worth monthly or quarterly at the very minimum. This may sound excessive, but being in tune and seeing even small movements in the right direction can help reaffirm your commitment and keep you focused.

The following page contains a form that will help you calculate your current net worth. You can make copies of this form or download a free copy by going to www.WealthBuilderLifestyle.com/tools.

The provided form is just one simple tool that can be a great gauge for accurately measuring your wealth. Think about this. Your car has numerous gauges just to tell you how it's doing, right? So doesn't it make sense that you would have a way to gauge and monitor one of the most important aspects of your life? Once you get in tune with your money, you will be amazed at how easy it is to hold on to and grow it.

Net Worth

Use the upcoming balance sheet to determine your net worth. Don't stress if you can't come up with a totally accurate amount for each category, just do the best you can. That being said, don't skip this task!

NOTES :

_____

_____

_____

_____

_____

PART ONE: CURRENT WEALTH STATUS

Current Net Worth

Assets (what you own)		Liabilities (what you owe)	
Property		**Property**	
Primary Residence	$_____	Primary Residence	$_____
Other Real Estate	$_____	Rental/Other Mortgages	$_____
Planes, Boats, RVs	$_____	Planes, Boats, RVs	$_____
Vehicles	$_____	Other Real Property	$_____
Misc. Personal Property	$_____	Other	$_____
Furnishings	$_____	Other	$_____
Other	$_____	Other	$_____
Total Property	$_____	**Total Property**	$_____
Investments (security)		**Short-Term**	
IRA	$_____	Credit Cards	$_____
Bonds	$_____	Other	$_____
401K	$_____	**Total Short-Term**	$_____
Mutual Funds	$_____	**Total All Liabilities**	$_____
Stocks	$_____		
Other	$_____		
Total Security	$_____		
Investments (growth)			
401K	$_____		
Mutual Funds	$_____		
Stocks	$_____		
Other	$_____		
Total Growth	$_____		
Investments (business)			
Investment Property	$_____		
Other	$_____		
Other	$_____		
Total Business	$_____		
Savings (liquid assets)		**Total Net Worth**	
Savings Accounts (cash)	$_____	Total Assets	$_____
Metals	$_____	Total Liabilities	$_____
Other	$_____	**TOTAL NET WORTH**	$_____
Total Savings	$_____	(assets – liabilities = net worth)	
Total All Assets	$_____		

RETIREMENT PROGRESS CHART

Once you have established an accurate net worth, compare your net worth to the ideal wealth progress amount for your age group below. These numbers are here just to give you an idea of minimums you really want to be at in order to stay on track and reach the million dollar milestone.

\multicolumn{6}{c}{Ideal Retirement Minimums}					
Year	Balance	Year	Balance	Year	Balance
21	$3,815	36	$128,349	51	$542,802
22	$7,771	37	$143,977	52	$568,318
23	$12,152	38	$160,966	53	$595,121
24	$16,993	39	$179,420	54	$623,281
25	$22,333	40	$199,453	55	$652,872
26	$28,212	41	$221,187	56	$683,973
27	$34,676	42	$244,754	57	$716,666
28	$41,771	43	$270,294	58	$751,041
29	$49,550	44	$297,958	59	$787,191
30	$58,067	45	$327,908	60	$825,214
31	$67,383	46	$360,318	61	$865,216
32	$77,561	47	$395,375	62	$907,307
33	$88,670	48	$433,280	63	$951,606
34	$100,784	49	$474,247	64	$998,237
35	$113,981	50	$518,507	65	**$1,047,333**

Financial Stability

So, how did things look? Was your net worth as much as you thought it would be? Does your income adequately support your financial lifestyle?

NOTES :

_____

_____

MEETING NEEDS

Considering the current fulfillment of your human needs is one of the best ways to evaluate how you are doing financially. Some of these categories might not initially appear wealth-related, so here are a few examples that may help trigger the connection for you.

Sustenance

If your career or income is in doubt, you may be concerned you won't even be able to get by.

Connection

If you don't have a high enough income, you may not be able to afford the expenses related to spending time connecting with family and friends. Or worse yet, you may be putting these costs on credit cards.

Security

If you have very little saved and invested, you may feel on the edge and stressed out. You might even be worried that at any minute, you could start falling behind and losing the wealth you've already created.

Growth

If you are not contributing to a savings and investment plan, you may feel like your financial status is stalled and not getting any better. This can lead to feelings of hopelessness.

Significance

If you have not built an acceptable amount of wealth for someone your age, you may feel like you are failing and or even insignificant.

Esteem

If your income has remained low and you have not (and are not currently) building wealth, you may feel inferior and like the world is looking down on you.

Inner Peace

If you don't have decent income, a good security cushion, growing investments, and a reasonable accumulation of assets for your age, you probably feel uncomfortable and rarely relax with peace of mind.

PART ONE: CURRENT WEALTH STATUS

Considering the current fulfillment of your human needs is one of the best ways to evaluate how you are doing financially. Not everyone needs the same amount of wealth or wealth building conditions to adequately meet their needs. Some people are content driving an old car and living in a humble home, while others would feel like they are total financial failures in that same situation. Those two people are going to have greatly different criteria for meeting their needs, and neither one is right or wrong. Everyone is wired differently, so we must all create a life that meets our own personal needs.

In the applicable areas below, enter ratings of 1 to 10 with 10 indicating you are fully meeting your needs in that category at present.

How well are you meeting your Seven Human Needs in each area?						
Sustenance	Connection	Security	Growth	Significance	Esteem	Inner Peace

NOTES :

___
___
___
___
___
___
___
___
___
___
___
___
___
___
___

PART TWO:
TWELVE MONTH REBALANCE

RISK CONSIDERATIONS

Now that you have captured all of your current data, we need to setup some initial rules. Things like your age, whether you currently own or rent, how many kids you have, your marital status, and current income all greatly affect your strategy. These factors will influence your best plan of action for moving forward. Here are a couple example situations that we can compare for a closer look:

Single, 25, no kids

If you are 25, single, and have no kids, you have few limitations and the consequences of your actions are pretty low risk. If you lose your job (or everything you own, for that matter), you can probably sleep on a friend's couch and have plenty of time to recover. Alternatively, if you make some high-risk, high-reward moves, you may launch yourself into wealth at an early age.

Married, 40, with kids

If you are 40, rent your home, live in a single income household, have two teenage kids, and have limited savings, you are what I call high risk. If you lose your job, your family could end up homeless. Few people could easily take you in. You may need to move, change your kid's school, or worse just to recover. It would be a bad situation to say the least. In this type of situation, one wrong step could cause a lot of pain, so we need to be sure to do as much as we can to ensure that doesn't happen. Taking a high-risk, high-reward gamble at this point could be financially and mentally devastating, and the financial loss would likely be far easier for you to get over than the emotional trauma.

Calculated Risk

The following tools are going to give you recommendations based on the Wealth Builder Lifestyle method. These are only recommendations, and you need to make sure that they make sense for you. I personally like low-risk, high-reward situations, but then again there are no guarantees in life. If you work to protect yourself from every risk you may never be able to afford any opportunities to build wealth. You must find your own successful balance.

I believe you need to take calculated risks if you want to be rewarded. I also believe in hoping for the best but planning for the worst. I won't take on any potential upside if I'm not prepared and willing to suffer the downside.

PART TWO: TWELVE MONTH REBALANCE

Just keep in mind that if you are not building wealth, you are choosing a life of voluntary enslavement. You will always be owned by the people you have to pay to exist. The only way to truly be free is by obtaining a level of wealth that allows you to afford your own freedom. If you put off building wealth for absolute security today, you will run out of time and be at the mercy of your owners in the long run.

As the cost of everything goes up (food, taxes, parking, rent, insurance), we have nothing left to dedicate to building wealth. This leaves us just working to exist without any luxuries or real freedom. This loss of freedom and opportunity has not come at the point of a gun, but unfortunately out of our own doing. Only we have the power to stop it.

NOTES :

THE BOMB - INCOME ALLOCATIONS

You may not initially be able to meet all the program guidelines for your income allocations. That's not only okay, it's to be expected. These are your first set of goals, and this program is designed to help you work towards and then *eventually* meet them. The Wealth Builder Lifestyle front-loads your wealth building strategy in order to maximize your long-term results.

Regardless of your income, these program principle goals will put you in a wealth building scenario. Each step you take from where you are towards being in line with these principles will make you a stronger wealth builder. It doesn't matter if you are currently going backwards, spending more than you are earning, or how much (if anything) you are saving and investing. Each step you take from here is a wealth builder step.

One thing is for sure: you're going to find out where you stand, which way you're currently moving, and how fast. After that's established we will work to shift you into a more powerful wealth building position. Small actions lead to big results, so don't get discouraged if your plan looks like a huge, insurmountable set of tasks. It may seem impossible for you to transition to a Wealth Builder Lifestyle, but have faith. You can absolutely do it.

NOTES :

___
___
___
___
___
___
___
___
___

PART TWO: TWELVE MONTH REBALANCE

Enter your total annual income (multiply monthly income from page 39 times twelve) in the form below to determine your income distributions.

Program Income Distribution Guidelines			
Select distribution percentages based on your income level.			
Annual Income	Level 1	Level 2	Level 3
$_____ Category	Up to $50,000	$50,000 to $150,000	$150,000 and above
Security Cushion Goal (percentage of income)	70%	60%	45%
Housing Expenses	45%	35%	25%
Necessity Expenses	15%	12.5%	10%
Personal Expenses	10%	10%	10%
Security Investments	10%	10%	15%
Growth Investments	10%	15%	15%
Business Investments	5%	10%	15%
Fun Money	5%	7.5%	10%
Short-Term Debt Payoff	(Varies)		
Reduce personal expenses and then investments to cover short-term debt payoff.			

As your income grows, so will the amount of each allocation. Over time it will become increasingly easier to meet these goals. Once you start investing, your investments will begin to create additional income which will contribute to your overall income.

Buckle down, be wise, and make sure this is a time of great prosperity for yourself and your family. There will be time to play when things stabilize later, but for now just get busy building wealth.

Your Income Allocation Totals

Take the percentages from the previous form that match your current income level and enter them in the following worksheet. Enter your net combined monthly income in the adjacent column and then multiply your monthly income by the percentage for each category.

You will need to start by determining the percentage required to pay the minimum payments on your current short-term debts. Then, reduce the Personal Expenses and long-term investment categories (followed by any others) as needed to balance all of the categories. For example, let's assume your net income is $2,000 and you have $150 in credit card debt you need to pay each month. Use this formula to determine the percentage of your income that needs to be dedicated to short-term debt. Divide the $150 by $2,000, then multiply that answer by 100 to determine the percentage: $150 ÷ $2,000 = 0.075. By multiplying that value (0.075) by 100, you can find the required percentage is 7.5%.

Current Program Income Distribution Guidelines			
Distribution Category	Your Percentages	Net Monthly Income	Monthly Allowance (income × percentage)
Example Category	20% ×	$2,000 =	$400
Housing Expenses	____% ×		$ _____
Necessity Expenses	____% ×		$ _____
Personal Expenses	____% ×		$ _____
Security Investments	____% ×	$ _____ =	$ _____
Growth Investments	____% ×		$ _____
Business Investments	____% ×		$ _____
Fun Money	____% ×		$ _____
Short-Term Debt Payoff	____% ×		$ _____
Grand Total (be sure not to exceed 100%)			$ _____

Have you caught your breath yet? You're probably wondering what you were thinking, wanting to retire a millionaire. In the following pages we will work through a multi-faceted, twelve month transition plan that will get you from point A to point B.

Once you get some time under your belt implementing these strategies, you will start to see dramatic improvements in your financial situation. These initial improvements will show up and be the most apparent in your net worth, especially if you are starting from zero and have never had any investment accounts before.

Saving and investing may seem out of your league but amazingly, in these financially complex times it has actually never been easier.

Where to Apply These Allocations

Meeting these goals will likely require some initial lifestyle adjustments. Just remember, we are talking about changing a life from one that spends the last 20 to 30 years struggling stressfully to one of financial security and comfort. The assurances provided by being financially sound should easily offset the initial discomfort. Here is the breakdown of what these allocations specifically cover.

PART TWO: TWELVE MONTH REBALANCE

Housing Expenses

This allowance will be used to cover your rent or home loan payments and other direct housing-related expenses like insurance, maintenance, and so on.

Necessity Expenses

All utility, phone, auto, grocery, child, health, disability, and insurance costs are included in this category.

Personal Expenses

These funds will be used for all your personal expenses such as haircuts, gym memberships, higher education, clothing, short-term loans, and any other personal items.

Security Investments

These investments should include low-risk assets like real estate, safer mutual funds, Certificates of Deposit, and possibly even a 50/50 allocation in cash and precious metals. Your goal is to try to get a safe 7% return. You should maintain enough of these in fairly liquid assets for use as your security cushion.

Growth Investments

This allocation will go towards higher return investments which may be less liquid and have higher potential risks. These will likely include growth, income, and international mutual funds as well as other investments that are not overly risky but have potential for returns in excess of 10%.

Business Investments

These funds may be used to invest directly in your own business or other companies. These will have higher anticipated returns in excess of 15% and (inherently) higher risk.

Fun Money

This is your reward. After all, all work and no play is no way to live. It's important that you actually spend this money to reward yourself or your family for following your plan. Don't try to be a superstar and invest or save this money. It may sound silly, but you have a far higher chance of failure if you don't focus this money on a fun reward because you could end up burning yourself out.

Short-Term Debt Payoff

Our goal is to get you to carry little to no short-term debt, especially in the early stages. Initially, you'll probably need to divert money from other areas in an amount that is adequate to meet your debt-reduction plan total. We will determine that exact amount later.

There may come a time when you need to violate the recommended percentages and reallocate some funds to balance your finances, and that's ok. But try to avoid it as much as possible. The problem created by repeatedly moving the boundaries is that they begin to lose their strength and you can actually start to develop new bad habits (and that works against our intention of creating positive Wealth Builder Lifestyle habits).

Shock Reduction

These days, a large percentage of our population is living closer and closer to the edge, if you find yourself a part of that statistic, don't be too hard on yourself. It should come as no surprise these days as we are bombarded with powerful, psychologically-driven advertisements and social pressure to appear wealthy (regardless of whether we actually are). This keeps us in debt and spending money rather than investing and doing the things that actually lead to being truly wealthy.

With so little emphasis placed on good financial education, most people are not prepared to fight off all the powerful forces pursuing their dollars. These efforts are in full force, coming from all angles—businesses, family, friends, and even the government. As your income and spending go up, the revenue the government earns through taxes automatically increases. Yet the government continues to raise tax rates to cover their poor financial habits. This continues to reduce the amount of money we have available to invest and spend, so we need to earn more and more just to stay in the same spot. If you're not actively growing your income and investments, you'll inevitably fall behind.

One of the great things about the Wealth Builder Lifestyle is that it not only focuses on solid spending and investment strategies but it also provides you with multiple strategies for career development and career income growth. By incorporating accelerated career income growth into your Wealth Builder Lifestyle you can put your overall wealth creation into hyper drive.

It's easy for people to fall into certain careers or feel like they have no other opportunities. This is where a mentor can help open your mind to new ideas. Taking action on a good career development plan can almost immediately lead to increased income, creating substantial increases within one to two years and having a tremendous effect on your lifetime earning potential.

PART TWO: TWELVE MONTH REBALANCE

I have personally used the same strategies I'm going to share with you to increase my own income multiple times by large percentages (and even doubled it a few times). I certainly can't guarantee these results for you, but I also never would have thought them possible for me—that is, until I met my unintentional mentor. Since I grew up poor, I was not naturally in an environment of wealth and thus had no idea how the real world of money worked. I got lucky and met a guy that had the skills necessary for life and career advancement who would eventually become a great friend and (ultimately) an unintentional, life-long mentor.

You see, I was raised up under the idea that you had to work hard for your money (and hard usually meant difficult physical labor). I still believe you have to work hard, but there is much more to it these days. Today, what is far more important is the market value that your energy produces. When you learn to create value, you give yourself leverage to move up. Then you need the confidence to emanate that value so you can sell it when it counts. This may come from getting something you don't already have (such as professional training) or it may come from just understanding the true value you already hold. We'll get into that more shortly.

NOTES :

_____
_____
_____
_____
_____
_____
_____
_____
_____
_____
_____
_____

THE BOMB - INCOME ALLOCATIONS
Twelve-Month Rebalance Plan

We have done some initial investigation into your current financial situation, so now let's break that information down and create a realistic plan that can transition you from where you are to within the Wealth Builder Lifestyle principles.

The point of a twelve month rebalancing plan is to get the painful part of the system out of the way as soon as possible. If the sacrifices are ongoing, the chances of you sticking with it diminish drastically. That being said, taking an approach that is too discreet could potentially harm your chances by not stirring you up enough to keep you focused on the goal. The danger there is that it can allow you to slip back into old habits, leading to another failed attempt at lifestyle change. The more difficult the rebalancing period, the more necessary it was and the more you should be proud of the actions you're taking.

Like I mentioned earlier, I am someone that advises people to hope for the best and plan for the worst. The principles of the Wealth Builder Lifestyle are designed with that in mind. If things go great, your wealth will just grow faster. If, on the other hand, things go poorly, you will be prepared as well as is reasonably possible.

We will now work to establish your rebalancing plan, this will create a foundation and starting point for you to start building wealth from.

Enter the Total Income (all sources) you determined on page 39 in the boxes below.

Current Monthly Income		
Income	Gross Monthly Income (before taxes)	Net Monthly Income (after taxes)
Total Income (all sources)	$	$

NOTES :

_____

_____

_____

_____

_____

_____

_____

BAD HABIT ASSESSMENT

When it comes to building wealth, two of the hardest habits to control are how much you spend and how much you invest. We indulge in spending for instant gratification and put off investing while we wait for some mysterious future date when the time will be right.

Well, I've got the mysterious, fail-safe time you have been waiting for, and I'm going to finally reveal this once elusive secret: the time is **now!**

Complete the following two worksheets to determine how much of an adjustment you will need to make in each category. This will determine exactly what it will take to get from where you are currently to within the Wealth Builder Lifestyle guidelines. Most of this information you have already captured, so you can refer back to the corresponding pages listed below for your answers. As a note, we will initially use your Combined Minimum Payment Total for your short-term debt before determining how much money it makes sense to free up in order to accelerate paying these debts off.

Current Spending Expenses table -- Page 38.

Current Short-Term Debts table -- Page 42.

Current Savings and Investments table -- Page 44.

Current Program Income Distribution Guidelines table -- Page 59.

Spending Habits

In the following form, enter the actual amount you are currently paying and the principle guideline amount for each item in the corresponding columns and categories. To determine the net difference between what you pay towards each category and what the principle advises, use the following formula:

actual amount - principle guideline amount = net difference

Then add and subtract all the category totals to determine the cumulative net difference for all your spending categories.

Note: for your "Principle Guideline" and "Net Difference" you do not need to break down each item individually. These spaces have been provided as an option to help you better budget and focus in on individual areas that could be adjusted to help meet your overall guideline goals.

PART TWO: TWELVE MONTH REBALANCE

Spending Habits (Twelve-Month Rebalance)			
Housing Expenses	**Actual Amount**	**Principle Guideline**	**Net Difference**
Example	*$75.00*	*$100.00*	*$-25.00*
Home (rent or mortgage)	$_____	$_____	$_____
Property Taxes (if separate)	$_____	$_____	$_____
Home/Renter's Insurance	$_____	$_____	$_____
Maintenance/Other	$_____	$_____	$_____
Total Housing Expenses	$_____	$_____	$_____
Necessity Expenses	**Actual Amount**	**Principle Guideline**	**Net Difference**
Utilities (all combined)	$_____	$_____	$_____
Health Insurance	$_____	$_____	$_____
Disability Insurance	$_____	$_____	$_____
Term Life Insurance	$_____	$_____	$_____
Phone, Cable, Internet	$_____	$_____	$_____
Auto (all related expenses)	$_____	$_____	$_____
Groceries and Household	$_____	$_____	$_____
Child Care	$_____	$_____	$_____
Laundry, Other	$_____	$_____	$_____
Total Necessity Expenses	$_____	$_____	$_____
Personal Expenses	**Actual Amount**	**Principle Guideline**	**Net Difference**
Clothes	$_____	$_____	$_____
Education	$_____	$_____	$_____
Other	$_____	$_____	$_____
Total Personal Expenses	$_____	$_____	$_____
Fun Money	**Actual Amount**	**Principle Guideline**	**Net Difference**
Entertainment	$_____	$_____	$_____
Vacations, Travel, Gifts	$_____	$_____	$_____
Other	$_____	$_____	$_____
Total Fun Money	$_____	$_____	$_____
Net Surplus or Deficit	**Actual Amount**	**Principle Guideline**	**Net Difference**
Grand Totals	$_____	$_____	$_____

INVESTING HABITS

Enter the actual amount you are currently investing and the principle guideline amount for each item in the corresponding column for each category. To determine the net difference between what you invest in each category and what the principles advise use the following formula:

actual amount - principle guideline amount = net difference

Investing Habits (Twelve-Month Rebalance)			
Investments	Actual Amount	Guideline	Net Difference
Example	*$75.00*	*$100.00*	*$-25.00*
Security Investments	$	$	$
Growth Investments	$	$	$
Business Investments	$	$	$
Total Investments	$	$	$
Short-Term Debt Payoff			
Short-Term Debt Payoff	$	$	$
Net Surplus or Deficit			
Total Investments and Debt Payoff	$	$	$

    Complete the following recap using your category totals to create a simplified overview of your spending and investing habits. Then, add your spending totals to your investing totals to determine your combined net surplus or deficit. If your actual amount exceeds the principle guideline (which should equal your total income), then you are spending more than you are earning. Unless you have some great investments, you are likely eroding wealth monthly rather than increasing it.

NOTES :

_____

_____

_____

PART TWO: TWELVE MONTH REBALANCE

Spending and Investment Totals (Twelve-Month Rebalance)			
Spending	Actual Amount	Guideline	Net Difference
Total Housing Expenses	$_____	$_____	$_____
Total Necessity Expenses	$_____	$_____	$_____
Total Personal Expenses	$_____	$_____	$_____
Total Fun Money Spending	$_____	$_____	$_____
Total Spending (all categories)	$_____	$_____	$_____
Savings and Investments			
Total Savings and Investments	$_____	$_____	$_____
Total Short-Term Debt Payoff	$_____	$_____	$_____
Total Investments (all categories)	$_____	$_____	$_____
Net Surplus or Deficit			
Grand Totals	$_____	$_____	$_____

  You may feel like some of these exercises are redundant, but remember that we are trying to build familiarity with working with money and an acute awareness of your own personal financial situation. This will help you build a subconscious awareness of where you currently are and what you need to do to start living a successful lifestyle full of wealth building habits. Having this awareness and understanding greatly increases your chance for successfully creating lasting change.

  So far, we have really covered the basics via a general analysis of where you currently are compared to where you need to be to start habitually creating wealth. That is a great first step, but now we need to start looking for the easiest areas to make the most significant changes to get you onto the fast track. During the initial rebalancing phase, we are going to work primarily with things that you currently have direct control over and can change immediately. We will use these initial changes to leverage larger overall changes that will get you in your best possible position for maximum lifetime wealth creation.

FINANCIAL SECURITY INSURANCE

Use the following forms to calculate some risk variables based on the Wealth Builder Lifestyle. All the options we will be looking at have merit, but the question of whether or not you can afford to purchase them (and when each choice makes sense) is one you'll have to answer yourself.

Health Insurance

The idea of health insurance is great—and in a perfect world we should all have it—but in reality if you are under 30 the likelihood of you having a medical need that makes it financially sensible goes way down (especially if you can't afford it while building wealth).

If you took the money that you would pay in premiums for insurance coverage from the age of 18 until 30and invested it, you would have a sizable investment. Unlike the fear-building political speak, in the unlikely event that you did have a medical expense you would likely have enough money to cover your expenditures out of pocket and in cash.

NOTES :

_____

_____

_____

_____

_____

_____

_____

_____

_____

PART TWO: TWELVE MONTH REBALANCE

In the following evaluation, the last amount (year 35) is based on just leaving the investment to grow after 12 years with no further contributions. The table below should help paint a more comprehendible picture and make it easier to understand the numbers behind health insurance. It gives a comparison of insurance premiums versus an equivalent investment at a 10% rate of return over time.

Health Insurance Versus Investment				
Premium Invested	$100	$150	$200	$250
Year 1	$1,264	$1,896	$2,528	$3,160
Year 2	$2,655	$3,982	$5,309	$6,636
Year 3	$4,184	$6,276	$8,368	$10,460
Year 4	$5,866	$8,800	$11,733	$14,666
Year 5	$7,717	$11,576	$15,434	$19,293
Year 6	$9,753	$14,629	$19,506	$24,382
Year 7	$11,992	$17,988	$23,985	$29,981
Year 8	$14,456	$21,683	$28,911	$36,139
Year 9	$17,165	$25,748	$34,330	$42,913
Year 10	$20,146	$30,219	$40,292	$50,364
Year 11	$23,424	$35,137	$46,849	$58,561
Year 12	$27,031	$40,546	$54,062	$67,577
Year 35	$242,044	$363,061	$484,088	$605,105
Insurance Purchased	This one is easy to calculate. Your return will always be $0!			

While you age and become more likely to develop medical needs, your account is growing into a more sizable and capable fund. The odds say that you would end that time period with most (if not all) of your investment in tact, a great head start at building wealth. If you take the opposite approach and pay the premiums, at the end of 12 years you will have nothing. I'm not telling you which way to go, I just believe in people having good, unbiased information and then making their own decisions.

Who Wants to Be a Millionaire?

Those are real, achievable numbers that any financial expert can verify for you. Keep in mind that I've only outlined twelve years of making contributions, accounting for just letting it sit and grow for the rest of the time. So by the time someone is 30, they could have this seed planted and be setup with a great start on a fully-funded retirement without any further contributions.

FINANCIAL SECURITY INSURANCE

If you took that same $250 premium and paid it from age 20 until 65 (essentially what you will do when buying insurance, although your insurance rate will shoot way beyond that as you age) the total investment you would have at 65 would be $2,271,836. I know, I know, we need to figure some medical costs in there, but come on—I'm sure you can afford it.

The following Health Insurance Evaluator will be very controversial because recommending someone at age 50 go without insurance won't sit well with some. I truly wouldn't want to see anyone at age 50 without health insurance, but I think that having less than $100,000 in net worth at that time is a far bigger risk to your wellbeing than not having health insurance.

Check your age, income, and net worth for a specialized recommendation. The calculations are based on an individual. If you are a couple, double all of the variables. If your recommendation is Ins./**Inv.**, refer to the "Retirement Progress Chart" on page 49. If you find that you have reached or exceeded the ideal retirement progress for your age, get insurance, if you are still below it you should consider investing.

Health Insurance Evaluator					
Income	Net Worth	Age 18 to 30	Age 30 to 40	Age 40 to 50	Age 50+
Less than $50,000	Less than $50,000	Invest	Invest	Invest	Invest
	Over $50,000	Insurance	Ins./**Inv.**	Ins./**Inv.**	Ins./**Inv.**
$50,000 to $150,000	Less than $50,000	Invest	Invest	Invest	Invest
	$50,000 to $150,000	Insurance	Ins./**Inv.**	Invest	Invest
	Over $150,000	Insurance	Insurance	Ins./**Inv.**	Ins./**Inv.**
Over $150,000	Less than $150,000	Insurance	Ins./**Inv.**	Invest	Invest
	Over $150,000	Insurance	Insurance	Ins./**Inv.**	Insurance

Kids should always be insured if possible. For low income families, there are usually government programs available at low or no cost. Regardless of whether you follow this guideline or not, enter your anticipated monthly premium below (if you plan to carry health insurance). You can get an estimated premium online if needed.

Monthly Health Premium	$

Disability Insurance

In the event you are unable to work due to a sickness or injury, disability insurance can provide some assurance that you will be able to continue paying your bills while maintaining your lifestyle. The premiums for this type of insurance typically run between 1 to 3% of your annual income. There are two scenarios when this type of insurance has substantial value.

Limited Cash Reserves

If you are financially close to the edge (meaning you do not have enough money in your security cushion to cover all your expenses for at least six months), this type of insurance may be a great option for you. If nothing else, it may be a good temporary fallback plan until you can adequately fund your security cushion.

Sole Provider

If you are the sole provider for your family and you get injured, you could put your family's livelihood at risk and potentially cause stress and hardship that could've easily been avoided.

If you aren't prepared to cover your expenses in the event of an emergency, you may also be putting your assets at risk with the potential to lose more than just your income. Consider this. If you have a $200,000 home with a mortgage balance of $125,000, you have $75,000 in equity. Should you fall behind and miss a few months of payments, your bank has the legal right to foreclose on your property. This means you could not only lose your home but also that $75,000 in equity.

This same situation could also come into play on any other assets that you currently have loans on. If you are considering getting disability insurance, take some time to review all your current loans. Some credit cards and other loans may already include coverage for your payments in the event of a disability. **Note:** if this is an optional feature they're going to charge you for, it's usually less expensive to cover this risk with a separate umbrella disability insurance policy. Don't make the pricey mistake of insuring these risks with multiple layers of coverage.

FINANCIAL SECURITY INSURANCE

The length of time you will receive coverage will depend on whether you get a short- or long-term policy. You'll want to make sure that your coverage will extend at least long enough to give you adequate time to sell or make other arrangements to protect your assets.

You can easily find places online that can give you a quote for this type of insurance. That being said, if you are seriously considering this insurance, I advise talking to someone in person before you purchase it. That way you can make sure you fully understand the coverage you will be receiving.

You will want to make sure you get at least enough coverage to pay your monthly minimum expenses. Then determine the duration of time you would like to be protected for.

If you will be obtaining disability insurance, enter your anticipated premium here:

| Monthly Disability Premium | $ _____ |

NOTES :

_____
_____
_____
_____
_____
_____
_____
_____
_____
_____
_____
_____
_____
_____
_____

PART TWO: TWELVE MONTH REBALANCE

Term Life Insurance

If you or your spouse are unfortunate enough to suffer a tragedy, term life insurance can be a huge relief. It's relatively inexpensive and can make a world of difference in a bad situation.

If this type of coverage makes sense for you, use the following formula to determine your Wealth Builder Lifestyle guideline for term life insurance. The word "estate" in the chart below means that you have a reasonable amount of assets that need to be protected or paid off to keep your estate settlement safe and simple.

Term Life Insurance Evaluator						
Description	Single no kids or estate	Single kids or estate	Married single income	Married dual income	Enter Children	Total Coverage
Income	N/A	$_____	$_____	$_____	N/A	Combine all column totals to determine amount of coverage.
Quantity	1	N/A	N/A	N/A	_____	
	×	×	×	×	×	
	$25,000	5	10	5	$100,000	
	=	=	=	=	=	
Category Total	$_____	$_____	$_____	$_____	$_____	$_____

The total you came up with working through this form is what I believe to be a safe amount of coverage. Single individuals with little to no assets really don't have a big need for coverage. The reason I still believe this is a good idea is due to the fact that it's very affordable. Plus, in the event of a death you would not be adding a financial burden onto others (who will already be enduring a terrible situation).

If you will be obtaining term life insurance, enter your anticipated premium here:

Monthly Term Life Premium	$_____

"There's nothing sexy about finance and numbers, but being wealthy will sure make you look and feel way more sexy!"

— Daniel Hartjoy

FINANCIAL SECURITY INSURANCE

Insurance Summary

Insurance can be great when you need it, but it's also a product. Companies tend to want to sell it to everyone, often regardless of whether it is in the purchaser's best interest or not. It is up to us as individuals to be informed consumers and make our own best decisions.

Based on the decisions you made on the last few pages, enter all your monthly premiums in the next form. Then combine your health, disability, and term life insurance premiums and enter the total.

Monthly Insurance Premiums	
Health Insurance	$
Disability Insurance	$
Term Life Insurance	$
Total Monthly Premiums	$

Security Cushion

As much as we may want to get aggressive paying off your debt and getting your money working for you, it would be foolish to do this with reckless abandon. I know many people that live right on the edge with no cushion for life's little surprises, and that's not a wise decision.

So, regardless of how much wealth you have, you need to have a plan in place to avoid being put into that type of situation. Keep in mind, when you are down and have something like this come up people and banks will abandon you without a second thought. If you lose your income or have another financial hardship, your ability to borrow your way out of it will likely vanish as quickly as the problem arose.

Ultimately you will want to build a fully funded twelve month security cushion, but for now let's just make sure you have at least a bare minimum cushion in place. I strongly recommend you have and maintain at least one month of your minimum expenses in cash or other liquid assets that you do not touch.

Enter the amount of your minimum monthly expenses from page 68 in the box below:

| One Month Security Cushion | $ |

PART TWO: TWELVE MONTH REBALANCE

If you already have enough set aside to cover your one month security cushion, great! Leave that alone and don't touch it. If, on the other hand, you don't, we need to create a plan to build that cushion over the next twelve months while still freeing up money to accelerate your short-term debt payoff.

Use the following worksheet to determine the amount you need to set aside each month to build your security cushion. This should be done simultaneously with the scheduled debt reduction, not one now and then the other later.

Follow the steps below to determine the monthly amount to set aside for your security cushion.

Security Cushion Calculator (Twelve-Month Rebalance)			
Enter Amounts	**Description**		**Monthly Security Cushion Contribution**
$1,750.00 - $600.00 =	← One Month Security Cushion ← Current Cash or Liquid Assets		*Example*
$1,150.00	÷	12 =	$95.83
$_____ - $_____ =	← One Month Security Cushion (from above) ← Current Cash or Liquid Assets		Your Plan
$_____	÷	12 =	$_____

During the Twelve-Month Rebalance phase of the program, you may need to sacrifice some of the program's guideline investment contributions. This is necessary to make sure that you substantially reduce or eliminate your short-term debt and build up your security cushion. We don't want to totally eliminate your investment contributions because we are trying to establish well-balanced Wealth Builder Lifestyle habits (so the sooner we make investments a habitual part of your lifestyle the better).

By repeatedly taking good financial actions, you'll be building habits that will allow you to create a lasting Wealth Builder Lifestyle. What takes conscious thought and sacrifice today will become your natural response in time, which will in turn keep your wealth growing by default.

SPENDING ALIGNMENT

We as individuals don't have the luxury of demanding more income when we spend too much so we are actually going to need to make some cuts. These cuts will allow you to pay off your debt and invest more. In the long run this will lead to more income and less debt. Wow, what a novel concept! Be prepared, the austerity riots are coming.

Fun Money

This may be one of the hardest areas to reduce your spending because fun money spending is often used to cope with the stresses of life. It's important to enjoy life and reward yourself. You work hard and make all kinds of sacrifices and deserve to be rewarded for your efforts.

The Wealth Builder Lifestyle's method of getting your fun money spending in balance is to set a budget and stick to it. Sounds easy, right? I'm joking! The way I recommend people successfully do this is by taking your fun money out in cash from every paycheck so that it's not mixed in with your other funds.

So forget what you were spending before and replace that amount with the guideline amount in cash—no less, no more. You may feel some initial shock as you adjust, but the beauty of this method is that after the first time you run short and have to pass on doing something you really wanted to do, you will start paying much closer attention to how you spend. The next time you take your fun money allowance, you are going to value it more and in turn make sure that you are getting the maximum amount of enjoyment out of every dollar.

Discretionary Spending Cuts

What are your discretionary spending habits? List the typical daily expenses that you could eliminate. This could include eating out, purchasing unnecessary drinks or snacks, fueling up for errands you don't actually need to run, and so on. Put it all down. Don't worry, it may not be necessary for you to give all of these up, but nixing or limiting some of them may help you balance things out in the short run.

Our goal is to be able to cut some of your discretionary spending to hopefully not only get you within the guidelines, but to also free up some extra money each month to pay down your high-interest, short-term debt. Keep that goal in mind as you grit your teeth about what you're considering giving up.

PART TWO: TWELVE MONTH REBALANCE

Use this form to enter any potential discretionary spending cuts you can think of. This is an exercise to evaluate as many options as you can come up with. You will make an actual list of the things you are going to cut later, so don't hold back now. For now, list all the items you could easily eliminate by simply making a different decision.

Multiply the amount of times a month you make this purchase by the cost to determine your monthly total.

Discretionary Spending Cuts		
Expense	Daily Expenditure	Monthly Total
1.	$	$
2.	$	$
3.	$	$
4.	$	$
5.	$	$
6.	$	$
7.	$	$
8.	$	$
9.	$	$
10.	$	$
11.	$	$
12.	$	$
13.	$	$
14.	$	$
15.	$	$
16.	$	$
17.	$	$
18.	$	$
19.	$	$
20.	$	$
Total Discretionary Cuts	$	$

SPENDING ALIGNMENT

Necessity Expenses

What is truly a "necessity?" In America, we are truly masters of making everything a necessity we just *have* to have.

Be honest with yourself. Look at all the items you have that fall under the necessity expense category and come up with a list of things that you can and will cut to get within the guidelines. These items may not need to be totally eliminated, possibly just reduced. Work with your numbers until you get them inline or have cut everything that you possibly can.

In the list below, capture your necessity spending cuts including your action plan for making them and put it in ink. Some ideas might be to reduce your grocery expenses by shopping smarter or splurging less, changing your phone plan, getting rid of premium movie channels, unsubscribing from movie services, etc.

Necessity Spending Cuts	
Necessity Expense / Action Required	Monthly Total
1. _____ / _____	$ _____
2. _____ / _____	$ _____
3. _____ / _____	$ _____
4. _____ / _____	$ _____
5. _____ / _____	$ _____
6. _____ / _____	$ _____
7. _____ / _____	$ _____
8. _____ / _____	$ _____
9. _____ / _____	$ _____
10. _____ / _____	$ _____
Total Necessity Spending Cuts	$ _____

Enter the total of any reduction in necessity expenses you came up with below.

Total Monthly Cash Available (from reducing necessity expenses)	$ _____

PART TWO: TWELVE MONTH REBALANCE

Personal Expenses

Personal expenses often have high emotional value. What does that mean? Well, many of these costs are for things like clothing, beauty products, higher education, and other items that make us feel better about ourselves. Eliminating these items just to save a dollar can lead to us being financially worth more but also to feeling less confident and unsure of ourselves. Be sure to maintain a good, honest balance between the two.

If you are not already under budget for this category, look closely at the personal expenses on your discretionary spending list. Thoughtfully go through these expenses to see how essential the things you spend money on are. See if there are some items that you could eliminate, or maybe just find a more affordable way to obtain the same result.

Use this form to capture any personal spending reductions you will make.

Personal Spending Cuts	
Personal Expense / Action Required	Monthly Total
1. _____ / _____	$ _____
2. _____ / _____	$ _____
3. _____ / _____	$ _____
4. _____ / _____	$ _____
5. _____ / _____	$ _____
6. _____ / _____	$ _____
7. _____ / _____	$ _____
8. _____ / _____	$ _____
9. _____ / _____	$ _____
10. _____ / _____	$ _____
Total Personal Spending Cuts	$ _____

Enter the total of any reduction in personal expenses you came up with below.

Total Monthly Cash Available (from reducing personal expenses)	$ _____

DEBT REDUCTION AND INVESTMENTS

We are going to be working on growing your income and wealth in many ways. Some of these methods can produce fast wealth gains while others can provide more of a steady cash flow (more commonly referred to as simply "income"). Regardless of how much your income grows, these core principles need to be a part of your habits and always respected.

I don't believe in chasing pots of gold which can lead to neglecting more sure-fire wealth building methods, like practicing good financial habits. Living a lifestyle of chasing big gains (without heeding the wealth builder lifestyle principles) is a good way to end up broke later in life.

Use the worksheets below to determine the modified program investment allocations you will be using during your rebalance period. During these first twelve months, we will morph the ultimate principles into achievable steps that move you towards your goal. This plan will allow you to free up money to put your short-term debt to rest using the upcoming debt-reduction strategy. Wait to enter your revised housing amount until after you complete the exercises in the upcoming housing section beginning on page 119.

Adjusted Spending (Twelve-Month Rebalance)					
Spending Items	Current Amount	Potential Reduction	Revised Amount	Program Guideline	New Net Difference
Housing (page 68 and 119+)	$_____	$_____	$_____	$_____	$_____
Necessity (page 68 and 79)	$_____	$_____	$_____	$_____	$_____
Personal (page 68 and 80)	$_____	$_____	$_____	$_____	$_____
Fun Money (page 68)	Guideline Amount		$_____	$_____	$_____
Security Cushion (page 76)	Monthly Amount		$_____	N/A	N/A
Total Spending and Security Cushion Expenses			$_____	$_____	$_____

NOTES :

_____

_____

_____

PART TWO: TWELVE MONTH REBALANCE

Use the following form to easily subtract your total spending and cushion contributions from your monthly income. This will determine how much you can apply monthly towards debt reduction and investments.

Available Monthly Debt and Investment Funds (Twelve-Month Rebalance)	
Monthly Income (page 39)	$
Spending and Security Cushion (page 81)	− $
Total Monthly Balance	$

Debt Reduction Versus Investing

We will use some general weight principles to determine how much of your available money should go towards debt and how much should go towards investments. If you compare debt (with a 20% interest rate) to a possible investment (with a return of 10%), you'll find it obvious that you want to kill that debt first and as quickly as possible.

NOTES :

___
___
___
___
___
___
___
___
___
___
___

DEBT REDUCTION AND INVESTMENTS

Going over the following guidelines is important. Feel free to move these numbers around a bit if you feel comfortable to get the best results. Just make sure you are still getting that debt knocked down quickly and that you continue investing. Redo the calculations every twelve months until your debt is gone.

Debt and Investment Calculator (Twelve-Month Rebalance)			
Total Debt (page 42)	Total Income Balance After Expenses (previous page)		Months Required to Pay Off Debt
$ _____ ÷	$ _____		= _____
Option 1: If total months to pay off debt is less than 12, use the following formulas.			
Total Debt $ _____	Total Income Balance After Expenses ÷ 12 = Monthly Debt Payment		$ _____ − $ _____ =
	Monthly Total to Invest		$ _____
Option 2: If total months to pay off debt is between 12 and 24, use the following formulas.			
Total Income Balance After Expenses $ _____	×	0.70 = Monthly Debt Payment	$ _____
		Monthly Total to Invest	
	×	0.30 =	$ _____
Option 3: If total months to pay off debt is over 24, use the following formulas.			
Total Income Balance After Expenses $ _____	×	0.80 = Monthly Debt Payment	$ _____
		Monthly Total To Invest	
	×	0.20 =	$ _____
	Monthly Debt Reduction Payment		$ _____
	Monthly Investment Contribution		$ _____

PART TWO: TWELVE MONTH REBALANCE

Short-Term Debt Reduction

One of the best ways to grow wealth is to eliminate debt (which directly works against wealth building). Most short-term debt carries too high of an interest rate to make it worth having, so wealth builders eliminate it. You will create a debt reduction hit list that will help you strategize the elimination of your debt in the quickest and most cost-effective way possible.

As I mentioned in the beginning of this program, there are four ways to live life. Most people live in a state of just sustaining themselves. If you are not able to get your finances in line with the principles for your income, you may need to temporarily move into a state of sacrificing. Temporarily, sacrificing can help catapult yourself from just financially sustaining to financially growing. That's a huge step up, so if you can get yourself into that position in only twelve months you will be feeling optimistic and living a new lifestyle of wealth creation.

Hit List

The enemy deserves no mercy. Yep, time to go ahead and kill them. This enemy has been destroying lives for far too long. This is one death that requires no bloodshed. Nobody will feel bad about your actions, well—that is, except the bankers that you have been making rich all these years. Poor little banks! They will have to find a new sucker to suck dry of wealth.

Use this form to create a debt hit list targeted at super-charging your debt elimination. Combine your knowledge of the amount of income you have set aside for debt reduction with whichever of the following methods best suits your personal strengths to come up with a quick and effective debt-reduction plan.

There are three basic debt-reduction strategies commonly utilized: one will minimize the overall amount of interest you will pay; another specializes in rapidly freeing up financial resources and reducing the quantity of loans; and the third option is a blend of the two (which often works best for most).

Option One: Minimize Interest

Apply all your additional debt reduction money to the debt with the highest interest rate first. Then, continue on to the second highest, the third highest after that, and so on until they are all paid off. This is both the most cost effective and also the quickest way to pay off all your debts.

DEBT REDUCTION AND INVESTMENTS

Option Two: Loan Elimination

Pay off your debts beginning with the smallest balance first. Then, move on to the second largest, the third largest, and so on until they are all paid off. This is neither the most cost effective nor quickest way, but often helps keep people optimistic by providing quicker individual debt eliminations. This method can also be beneficial if you are very short on money each month as it will reduce your minimum expenses quicker by eliminating the payments from those smaller loans.

Option Three: Wealth Builder Lifestyle

By taking a mix of the above two options, this method can help free up cash *and* quickly eliminate the number of bills you have to pay each month. The benefits of this are that you get a rapid sense of accomplishment and an added safety net (because of the extra available cash) while still keeping the overall interest paid to a minimum. To use this method, use Option Two for up to six months to knock out some small loans quickly before transitioning on to Option One to avoid paying excessive interest. The following worksheet shows an example hit list based on Option Three: Wealth Builder Method.

Hit List (Hit Amount: $90)						
Creditor	Loan Balance	Minimum Payment	Hit List Payment	Hit Start Date	Payoff Date	APR
Example Loan 1	~~$600~~	$60	$150	1/1/2013	4/1/2013	*12%*
Example Loan 2	~~$1,250~~	$75	$225	5/1/2013	9/1/2013	*19%*
Example Loan 3	~~$500~~	$35	$260	10/1/2013	10/1/2013	*6%*
Example Loan 4	$5,000	$250	$510	11/1/2013	3/1/2014	*12%*
Initial Loan Total	$7,350			Yearend Balance	$1,530	

    You will find your own worksheet to fill in on the next page. To determine your total Hit Amount, subtract your Minimum Payment Combined Total (from Current Short-Term Debts form on page 42) from your Monthly Debt Reduction Payment (from the Debt and Investment Calculator on page 83). Continue by entering your current loans, balances, APRs, and minimum payments (and list them in the order you want to pay them off in, which should be based on the method you chose).

    To determine the Hit List Payment amount, add the Hit Amount to the Minimum Payment for your first target. Figure out how many months it will take at that rate to pay it off and from that determine the Payoff Date. The Hit Start Date will be the following month after you successfully pay off a debt. The hit start and payoff dates do not need to be exact. To

PART TWO: TWELVE MONTH REBALANCE

calculate the dates, just assume that 100% of each payment will be applied to the debt's principal and round up on the last month (to account for some interest expenses).

Now that the first loan is paid off, take that minimum payment and the Hit List Payment and add it the Minimum Payment for your next target debt. Continue down the list until you reach your last debt. You will have to do a little math to determine your yearend balance, especially if you have a large amount of debt or limited income to apply to debt reduction. If you need additional space, make some extra copies of this form and carry over your totals.

Hit List (Hit Amount $ _____)						
Creditor	Loan Balance	Minimum Payment	Hit List Payment	Hit Start Date	Payoff Date	APR
_____	$_____	$_____	$_____	_____	_____	____
_____	$_____	$_____	$_____	_____	_____	____
_____	$_____	$_____	$_____	_____	_____	____
_____	$_____	$_____	$_____	_____	_____	____
_____	$_____	$_____	$_____	_____	_____	____
_____	$_____	$_____	$_____	_____	_____	____
_____	$_____	$_____	$_____	_____	_____	____
_____	$_____	$_____	$_____	_____	_____	____
_____	$_____	$_____	$_____	_____	_____	____
_____	$_____	$_____	$_____	_____	_____	____
_____	$_____	$_____	$_____	_____	_____	____
Initial Loan Total $_____			Yearend Balance $_____			

It's easy to get excited about finally getting started on saving and investing. Everyone's enthusiastic about seeing positive asset growth! Unfortunately, forgetting about debt reduction can actually lead to going backwards financially, especially if your debts have higher interest rates than the anticipated returns on your investments.

DEBT REDUCTION AND INVESTMENTS
Do not incur more debt!

I know you may be feeling card-swiping withdrawals—you *have* been being good, right? Don't give in to the urges! Keep one or two credit cards handy for emergencies **only**. (And keep in mind, retail therapy is not an emergency!)

Debt, Spending, and Investment Summary

Enter the results from your previous calculations into the following form which you will use as a reference for the next twelve months on how, where, and when to allocate your income. It's important to setup your investment contributions to come directly out of your paycheck the day you receive it, if at all possible. On payday, immediately withdraw enough cash to cover your fun money and personal expenses so you are not tempted to use your debit or credit cards to pay for them. Setup automatic payments for your bills if possible so you can just make your deposit and forget about it.

The more isolated and separate you can keep these items, the better success you will have. Once everything is setup, you should rarely need to access your debit cards, credit cards, or checking accounts because your small, frequent transactions will be done in cash. When you're finished, make a copy of the following sheet so you can keep it handy.

NOTES :

_____

_____

_____

_____

_____

_____

_____

_____

_____

_____

PART TWO: TWELVE MONTH REBALANCE

Rebalance Summary

Spending I will reduce (or cut entirely) for the next twelve months:

Necessity Spending	Personal Spending
1. _____	1. _____
2. _____	2. _____
3. _____	3. _____
4. _____	4. _____
5. _____	5. _____
6. _____	6. _____
7. _____	7. _____
8. _____	8. _____
9. _____	9. _____
10. _____	10. _____

Expense Budgets

Item	Location to Keep Funds	Amount
Housing Expenses (page 81)	Checking Account	$ _____
Necessity Expenses (page 81)	Checking Account	$ _____
Personal Expenses (page 81)	Cash	$ _____
Fun Money (page 81)	Cash	$ _____

Security Cushion

Security Cushion (page 81)	Savings or Liquid Asset	$ _____

Short-Term Debt Reduction

Item	When to Pay	Amount
Debt Reduction (page 83)	Immediately Each Paycheck	$ _____

Investments

Monthly Investments (page 83)	Immediately Each Paycheck	$ _____
Total of All Expenses (should not exceed income)		$ _____

CAREER FAST-TRACKING

Thought you were in deep before? Well, now we are going to raise the bar. Better to aim higher than the mark, than to aim for the mark and come up short. If you come up a little short on the high target, you may still clear the bar. If you come up a little short when aiming to just barely clear the bar, you'll miss.

Ultimate Income Requirement

What is your current income? _____

Does this adequately meet your financial needs? Yes ____ No ____

How many hours a week does your career consume? (Travel, work at home, etc.) _____

Can you currently afford all the material goods and services you desire? Yes___ No___

What are the five most significant things (if any) you are lacking due to your current level of income?

1. _____
2. _____
3. _____
4. _____
5. _____

    Although we will always talk of keeping your debt down and watching your spending, we've no intention for you to have to live like a pauper all your life. Just the opposite, in fact. The main objective is to ensure you keep making progress on wealth building. You can't afford to sacrifice financial growth for momentary enjoyment. Most people put fun "in the moment" before wealth building and thus never get around to actually building the wealth. This doesn't work out in the long run and has harsh consequences that nobody wants.

    This exercise is to determine how much income you would need to live your ultimate lifestyle. Go ahead and find out how much you would need to earn to afford everything you really want. I advise you to be liberal here and just put it all out there. Most people hold themselves back financially because of unfounded personal beliefs about how much money they could earn, ultimately settling for far less than they are capable of achieving.

PART TWO: TWELVE MONTH REBALANCE

I'm speaking as a former "self-limiter." When my personal beliefs were shattered by someone who pushed me to do what I perceived as unthinkable, I was amazed at how much I could earn and how quickly I could change my income. It was a profound life-changing and eye-opening experience, one I hope I can help you create.

My Ultimate Lifestyle

To complete the My Ultimate Lifestyle worksheet, create a list of your ultimate desires and calculate just how much they would cost. It will be a big help if you have a calculator and the internet available so you can determine their actual cost and compute the necessary loan payments. It's not necessary to get overly detailed in adding the cents—just round numbers will do. Don't worry about how big the numbers get, just be honest about what you really want.

Work through the following form to determine the monthly expenses for your dream lifestyle.

My Ultimate Lifestyle					
Item	Total Costs	Monthly Payments	Monthly Insurance	Monthly Expenses	Monthly Totals
Home	$	$	$	$	$
Auto 1	$	$	$	$	$
Auto 2	$	$	$	$	$
Education	$	$	$	$	$
Boat	$	$	$	$	$
Motorcycle	$	$	$	$	$
RV	$	$	$	$	$
Travel	$	$	$	$	$
Vacations	$	$	$	$	$
Other	$	$	$	$	$
Other	$	$	$	$	$
Other	$	$	$	$	$
Grand Totals	$	$	$	$	$

So, what was your total? Was it higher or lower than you actually thought it would be? Hopefully you enjoyed just thinking about the fun you could have with all that stuff.

We are very fortunate to have so many opportunities available to us. Having big dreams and inspirational goals can be very motivating.

Enter the total monthly cost of your dream lifestyle below:

Ultimate Lifestyle Monthly Cost	$

Base Income Goal

As you setup your life to build wealth and enjoy the lifestyle you want, you need to know what kind of income you're actually going to need. If you have, for example, a $150,000 a year dream lifestyle and are in a career that has a top earning potential of $50,000, you have a big problem. This is a common predicament for people who pick their career before determining the cost of their desired lifestyle.

Use this form to get a ballpark calculation of the annual income you would need to live your ultimate lifestyle. Don't worry if it seems out of your reach. When you learn to live the Wealth Builder Lifestyle, money will be easier for you to obtain. Once you figure it out, wealth will become increasingly accessible and you will find that there are many ways to grow your prosperity outside of just your career.

Dream Lifestyle Income Calculator		
Dream Lifestyle Monthly Cost	(accounts for your taxes and investments)	Annual Income Need
$	× 2 = $	× 12 = $
This calculation leaves 50% of your income to cover your taxes, savings, and investment funds.		

So, how does your current income match up with your dream lifestyle cost? Does your current career have the potential to ever meet your dream lifestyle income requirement?

The next step in this program is going to take a serious look at your career in a number of ways. By doing so you can determine if there are changes that can be made within your current career that would allow you to increase your income, or you may discover a career change is in order.

Job Commoditization

As the ideas and products we once saw as new become known, their prices and the careers related to them go through a process I call "job commoditization." As with any commodity, over time we discover and incorporate every imaginable efficiency into the creation process and develop training programs to create an abundance of workers specializing in the specific skill sets required. As we move towards and reach that point, the item's unit cost goes down and pay rates stabilize (and often times even fall).

Take, for instance, the web design industry. When this industry first exploded, we had a huge demand for its services and few workers with the necessary skills (since it was a new technology). The people that had those skills were very valuable and in high demand. Over time we have trained an abundance of people to perform those roles while simultaneously improving the related technology used to create websites. What used to take serious coding knowledge (which few knew how to do) now has literally become "drag-and-drop" simple, requiring little to no coding at all. Therefore, while many spent money and time getting the education necessary to acquire those seemingly well-paid jobs, the pay started coming down due to the technological advances in web-building tools and the increased supply of qualified workers. Now there is an over abundance of people who can build websites, and it's only natural that the pay reflects it. Today, twelve-year-old kids can build high quality websites and skilled people are willing to do it for $10 an hour. Do you really want to compete with them to make a living?

This is the unfortunate state of the world we are living in. Things are changing at the speed of light, and if you're not changing with it, you will get left behind. This is why it's so important to be on top of your finances and have a solid plan.

Exporting of Jobs

You hear a lot of talk about overseas manufacturing and bringing those jobs back to the US. As good as that sounds, based on what I have just told you those jobs are often times no longer what they used to be.

It is impossible for the US to compete with overseas labor. Think about this: it used to be we could charge more for American-made products because the quality was superior to places like China and other foreign countries. But those days are long gone. China (as well as other countries) is now as good (or better) than us at manufacturing.

Take for example the iPhone and iPad. They are solid proof that some of the highest quality and most technologically advanced products are now successfully being made in China, a country once laughed at for producing low-quality junk. Do we want the high-tech jobs of manufacturing those products back? Maybe, but a lot of the high-tech work is done by high-tech machines, reducing the labor portion to a low-paying, virtually unskilled job.

If you want to succeed today, you really need to retrain your mind and sharpen your tools. Two things these international countries still struggle with are ideas and creativity. Those companies need to know *what* to make, so they turn to those who have the next great idea that will create the new markets and opportunities. We need something to reinvigorate our economic engines, and it's not likely to come in the known ideas of the past. We have major environmental issues that are not going to allow us to adequately grow our wealth and economies based on the consumption-based model that brought us this far.

The Rich and Poor Gap

Don't let yourself get distracted by the news, media, and politicians rousing anger about the rich and poor gap. It is there and growing—which is one of the primary reasons why I created this program—but getting upset or distressed about it is not going to help change your fate. Holding your breath and waiting for the Democrats or Republicans to fix it will get you nowhere, and that time spent waiting will put you even further behind.

What built the US and global economy at large is the freedom, creativity and drive of individuals. As long as you are willing to wait for a solution, the rich will continue to get richer and you will stay where you are or fall behind. Take the information in this program and put it to work. This is the same information the rich people use to get rich.

A word of caution, if you are a supporter of taxing the rich in some attempt to get their money passed down to you, take these few things into consideration. First of all, if you do take action and start to build your own wealth, you will run into the taxes you so desired, which will ultimately make it harder for you to get ahead. Secondly, the money will always leave those that don't understand it and return to those who do. So, the resulting outcome will be that this new obstacle will only make it harder for you while the rich will work around it and continue to successfully grow their wealth.

Once this new tax is in place, it will limit the ability for everyone to build wealth through investing. But the real loss will come to those with the least, since it will slow their growth potential. Don't look at the wealthy and try to create obstacles that will stop them from building wealth. Copy them, do the same things they do and you too will get the same results.

Career Fast-Tracking

We know it's more important than ever to make sure we maximize our income and do the right things with our money, so how do we do it?

Through positive role models and life experiences, I've been blessed to have my eyes opened to different "actualities." I say "actualities" here because I believe reality is totally changeable. If so, then there is essentially no such thing as definite reality—only what you believe reality will be.

PART TWO: TWELVE MONTH REBALANCE

I was able to greatly accelerate my career and income because I challenged what most people would accept as reality. I hope I can impact you in a way that will help you break down the walls created by your own beliefs. I believe we limit ourselves with what we believe to be the reality of what our future holds. When you challenge your beliefs you open up your life to endless opportunities—opportunities to try and do the things you never would have thought possible.

So if there is no such thing as reality (and consequently there is only the illusion of reality), why can't we just change it in any way we want? Well, who said you can't? If you believe something about your future is possible, your chances of it being true go up dramatically.

All right, so now you probably think I'm talking nonsense. I get that. So, let's talk about how this craziness can go from virtual reality to actuality.

Goal

You need to start with an income goal. You should have previously determined what your ideal income goal would be as well as what your current income needs are (enough to cover your essential investments and expenses). If you are not yet comfortable aiming for your ideal income, select something you are comfortable with that will exceed your current income needs by an amount that will excite and motivate you.

You can *absolutely* shoot for your ideal income right out of the gate, if you want. I'm a proponent of going large and aiming as high as you want. For some people, that approach may be inconceivable this early in their financial lifestyle transformation. For them, aiming too high too soon could lead to a feeling of being overwhelmed and result in discouragement, thus increasing the likelihood of falling out of the program. You will have to make the call based on your own personality type and take the approach that's right for you.

Regardless of where you set your goal today, I want you to certainly keep your thoughts looking out beyond that goal. For example, even if your compromise was a $100,000 income, I don't recommend going into a specialized field that has a $100,000 cap with no potential for growth towards your ideal goal.

You can't afford to think in the short term, especially considering how drastically things can change and that our most well-constructed plans can easily become obsolete before we ever reach our goals. I frequently run into people who got a lot of specialized training and then realized they don't even like the field they are in, or outsourcing or other changes eliminated the demand. At that point, they realize they have spent a bunch of money and time getting prepared for something that is no longer of value to them.

By thinking beyond your initial goal you can try to tailor your training, skills, achievements, and experiences to be diverse and applicable in multiple fields, reducing your chances of disappointment or a major setback.

Personal Fit

This is probably one of the most overlooked, yet absolutely essential items to fully maximizing your career and getting fulfillment out of it. You are going to dedicate a lot of your life (and some of your best years) to your career, so you want to make sure you will enjoy it. Work does not have to be about sacrificing.

If you really want to excel in any career or business, do something you love and have passion for. Passion comes a lot easier when you love what you do. This is a surefire way to make sure you can happily put your heart and soul into your career, which in the end will yield the maximum amount of fruits for your labor. If you want a happy and fulfilling life, go back and read the last two sentences again as it is a major key to that end. Today, our society really focuses on and revolves around money, but despite its essentiality, if you don't love what you're doing, no amount of money will bring you happiness doing it.

Time—not money—is the currency of life. You can make more money, but you can't make more time. None of us know how much time we have left, so we had better make the most of it and enjoy every moment to the best of our abilities.

Seven Things You Absolutely Need

So make sure your career or business pursuits involve something you really have a passion for. Below we will revisit the Seven Human Needs and how they absolutely affect the fulfillment you will get out of your career.

Sustenance

I don't believe in working just to sustain myself. When you get skills or training, you want to make sure you will always be broadly marketable. Make sure you will always be in demand to a level where you are certain you can sustain your base living and lifestyle.

Connection

Will this direction put you in a group of like-minded people that can positively complement and enhance your life? Will you be working with people that are of a caliber that you would want to build a relationship with and spend time around? This is important because most people spend at least a third of each weekday at work, so this will be a key source of building friends and relationships (which are essential components of a good life).

PART TWO: TWELVE MONTH REBALANCE

Security

Will this career give you financial security and peace of mind? Will it allow you to grow financially for a long period of time? Is it stable? And if not, will the skills and experience you obtain allow you to easily cross over to another career path while still maintaining your financial security?

Growth

Will you continue to grow and develop new skills? Does the industry have room for growth and innovation that will keep it relevant? Are you going to be able to achieve new goals and continually expand yourself through your efforts?

Significance

Will this path give you a feeling of significance? Will this job be rewarding in a way that makes you feel good about what you are doing? Doing something that adds value to other peoples' lives often leads to a feeling of significance. Earning a good income and having the respect of your peers can also lead to feeling significant.

Esteem

Will this career and work environment give you confidence and a sense of pride? Will it allow you to feel good about what you are doing and have done? Will you be able to excel and be looked upon as a great contributing asset?

Inner Peace

Ultimately inner peace is what we all need and strive for. It's what motivates us to pursue the fulfillment of all our needs. Will your career choice broadly serve your six other needs as well as give you the potential to meet your need for inner peace and fulfillment?

If your career can fulfill the general needs we all have, you are far more likely to feel fulfilled and enjoy what you are doing. This can help take the negative aspect of "work" out of earning an income and replace it with something far more pleasurable.

Overpriced Education

When evaluating any career advancement, it is important to analyze the expense of that perceived advancement. When an economy is struggling, people will often spend a lot of money and energy doing retraining and trying to advance their education. This is a great idea conceptually, but I have seen too many go at it blindly without figuring in the cost to make sure it will actually make sense in the long run.

It's important to take into consideration not only the cost of the training or schooling but also your lost income earning potential for that period of time. If well thought-out and properly executed, this can really increase your working years' income potential. If done wrong, it can put you in debt and become a waste of time. These days, this risk can be excessively high in many fields as job commoditization takes effect.

Make sure you look at the bigger picture when making your career training and education decisions so you can make sure that over the long run they make as much sense as they initially appear to. If you lose five years of income earning just for training, you had better make sure the increase in pay is virtually assured and will offset your education expenses, lost income, and bypassed investment opportunities by a decent margin. If the advancement opportunity you are looking into doesn't meet that criteria, you may want to think it through a little further and possibly take another path all together.

Education

I'm not sold on education, education, and more education in the same way many are. I think getting an education for a career makes sense, but only when it is specifically applicable and not as a general rule. I see more and more people coming out of college with no job prospects. They didn't have a set direction and didn't get any specific training that qualified them for anything in particular. They then enter the working world with a lot of debt, only to be disappointed by the lack of good job opportunities. That was not what they were sold on going in, and now after a lot of hard work and commitment they feel ripped off—and rightfully so.

I think one of the most substantial benefits that an employer gets from someone with a four-year degree is that they can easily see a level of commitment to pursue a better life in that worker. This is not to be underestimated by any means, and I think it's highly desirable, but a trait like that needs to be complimented with a bigger plan and an intention of getting somewhere specific (or an attainment of skills that are broadly marketable and sought after).

Today, a lot of people are going to vocational schools or getting specific training for certain careers. I think this route also needs to be well thought out if it's going to be successful. You are investing time, energy, and money into very specific training that may only be usable in one profession or career. This can often power you up and make you valuable to that specific industry, but also make you very vulnerable to job commoditization.

Depending on your career choice and goals, that may not be an issue. If the money is suitable to your lifestyle and it fulfills your needs, then it could be a perfect course and shortcut over the typical four-year degree. The downside is (and the reason this can lead to job commoditization) that because your skills are not necessarily valuable outside that specific market, your employer undoubtedly also knows that your options are limited. Consequently, this can allow them to keep your pay down without a high risk of losing you as their wealth building asset.

Make Good Career Decisions

We live in very fast moving and changing times. The paths of yesterday aren't necessarily going to fit within today's job market and societal demands. This is where it's critical for you to think about what you really want out of life financially, and, (even more importantly) your career environment and opportunities. There is no correct blanket decision that will work universally to lead someone towards a fulfilling, financially-rewarding, and prosperous career. We each have our own unique traits, desires, and talents, so we need to take the information available and personally decide our best course of action.

Financially

You need to consider the lost earning and investment cost when you pursue your education and make sure the sacrifice is worth the reward. This really needs to be done thoughtfully, looking way down the road. It's certainly a lot easier to get a higher education when you are young and unburdened, so don't skip it for the quick buck.

College

I think this is a great asset for attracting companies and giving them the confidence that if they invest their time and money into training you to fulfill their needs that you will stick around. This comfort can open the door to a lot of opportunities even without any trade-specific training. A degree is proof that you have committed to making your life better, which is an admirable and a desirable characteristic.

Trade-Specific Training

If you will be content in one specific industry or area of expertise, this can fast-track you towards higher earnings by quickly developing marketable skills. The risks to consider here are possibly outgrowing your career and potential changes in the industry you pick, which may put you at a disadvantage later in life.

CAREER FAST-TRACKING
Personal Skill Development

I think this is something everyone should work on regardless of where they are currently or where they want to go. A college degree may be able to open a door for you, but well-rounded personal skills will be what propel you rapidly to the top in anything you do. I think that this is the future of career development and marketability. In a society that is moving so fast, is so complex, and is changing by the minute, learning what you needed to know yesterday will be of little value.

The best way to prepare for that and to be of great value is to become well rounded. Some people are naturally well rounded because they picked up their skills from their environment or upbringing, while others have moderate to substantial weaknesses or holes in their personal skills. These holes can all be filled in, and there are a lot of specific courses available to focus on virtually any weakness in order to eliminate it. Not all of these skills can or will go on your resume, but they will certainly show up in your interview, your work performance, and overall ability to add value to a team.

The types of applicable personal skills are numerous: selling, managing, negotiating, communicating, team building, and so on. These skills are not universally taught to us along the way, but many of these key aspects will be mastered by and present in the most successful in life. For example, when I talk about selling, that doesn't just relate to a sales career. To get ahead in life, you will frequently have to successfully sell yourself.

Summary

In general, I don't think you can solely apply any one particular approach in order to succeed. If you truly want to be successful, your specific situation will likely require a blended approach. If you are in college and know a specific industry you want to go into, you may want to get a certification or take a trade school course simultaneously. That way when you hit the job market you are seriously prepared. This may require a little more thought and work on your behalf, but it could catapult your career ahead by years, making you more marketable and worthy of a higher starting salary.

These things apply regardless of your age, race, education, and experience. The later in life (or the more disadvantaged) you are the more critical it will be that you give these things adequate consideration and properly implement these concepts. Not only is it never too late, but **now is always the best time** to make your plans. Waiting is never a good idea.

PART TWO: TWELVE MONTH REBALANCE
Foresight and Anticipation

Regardless of whether you choose to grow your income via a business or by further career development, it is essential that you make every effort to foresee what is coming in the future. This is a skill too few have (or at least utilize).

Never in our history have things changed so fast. This creates many challenges for those that just want to relax and not have to think or strategize too much. It also creates continual opportunities for those who will step up, get informed, and think ahead. This puts the complacent non-thinker at a huge disadvantage and at the mercy of those who are embracing this new way of life.

If things move so fast, why should we invest the time and energy only to have what we are building become obsolete shortly after we get it to market? That is where the opportunity lies. You need to be building (or a part of the building of) the next best thing that nobody has heard of yet. Unlike in the past when businesses remained for a long time and owners would continually focus on perfecting what they were doing, now consumers are ready for the next thing before they figure out the last one.

Capitalizing on Chaos

With that in mind, you need to be looking forward. Businesses will be changing directions often, reinventing themselves, coming and going, and you need to fit into all that chaos and be of great value. All these gyrations really lead to the opportunities of the future. If businesses are coming and going on a three, four, or five year cycle then there will be a lot of value for someone who understands instant market penetration and extremely fast business growth. Just as important will be those that know how to wind down a business in the quickest and most profitable way. These are just two examples, food for thought of what opportunities may come and what the new career market may look like.

I think the days of traditional education and training are going by the wayside because by the time something is known well enough to be taught it could very well be obsolete. This is not meant to be taken as a blanket statement, as some sectors will remain long-term like gas, oil, healthcare, food, etc., and thus benefit from traditional educational paths. But within even these stable industries, there will be new shifts that will create opportunities. Those that find them and take action will prosper. The other option (for those that don't get up to speed and adapt) is the likely possibility of being commoditized and falling closer to or fully into poverty.

CAREER FAST-TRACKING
Business

This is the most commonly used method to build wealth quickly. That being said, it's not something that fits everyone's personality, lifestyle, and skills. Therefore, in my mind it's not the be-all and end-all solution to growing wealth. Many would disagree with this, and if you pay attention at all you will see many ads and offers about how to make a bunch of money running your own business.

I love business and have been in it most of my adult life. I also believe it will hold the most opportunities for building substantial wealth in the foreseeable future. But that doesn't mean it will be easily available to the average person or right for everyone.

Right now in the US the laws and regulations in place are so burdensome that it's almost impossible to be a small business and comply with them all. This extra challenge leads to many failures of small businesses and even more that never get started. This reduces competition for the big guys, which leads to a few ultra-wealthy large corporations and many would-be business owners having to take lower paying jobs at these larger companies.

Having said that, in the near future many may have to enter the business world and become experts at figuring all this out just to find a decent financial opportunity. Below are a few things to take into consideration if you are thinking about starting a business.

Stress

Unless you have ran a business before, you are probably underestimating the amount of stress that can be involved. Keeping up with government regulations, cash flow, taxes, employees, and so on can be an overwhelming task sometimes.

Free Time

Most people see successful business people and think, "Wow, it must be nice. They come and go as they please, taking long vacations to great destinations." Those are perceptions based on looking from the outside in at a successful business. But in reality there are many businesses that are just getting started, don't have enough cash flow, are in a growth mode, or are currently transitioning (which leaves the owner with little to no free time). They may actually be stressed out and working around the clock.

Passion

Many people start a business for the money, but I have learned not to look at the money first. If you don't enjoy what you're doing, no amount of money will ever be enough to make it rewarding. To have passion, your business needs to meet your needs. When you have passion, obstacles that might otherwise seem insurmountable will be powered through with confidence. When you have passion, you will not easily accept failure, and success will at times even seem effortless.

Confidence

Regardless of whether you have it right now, you need to get and maintain your confidence. Whether you are running a business or are an employee, in a fast-moving, ever-changing society, there will be numerous opportunities to have self-doubt and question your abilities.

There are some good programs out there that can help you develop confidence and interpersonal skills. These are very essential skills for success and are aspects of our lives that are changeable, so work to be the best you can at them.

Buck the Trend

Don't be afraid to "buck the trend" and go against what others say or think. Taking an alternative path often opens up new opportunities and in an economic time when those are limited doing something different may be your saving grace. I'm not saying to do the opposite of something just to be different, but if you can find a way to do something better or add some additional value to a situation, you will be deserving of more.

Taking the road less traveled or cutting in a new path may be met with skepticism and concern from family, friends, and others we may trust and look to for guidance. Listen to their advice, test it against your plan, and then move forward accordingly. But honestly, when you venture into the unknown there will be few that can give you "good advice" because they too lack experience in the area and *that* is exactly where a lot of opportunity lies. The fact that it's unknown will keep a lot of people from discovering it, and most that do will lack the confidence to take the risk on something unproven.

Job Change

In the past, a job change was a great chance to accelerate income growth. Although possibly a higher risk proposition these days, I still believe it can be a wonderful opportunity, especially if you have unique or exceptional skills in an area with high demand. As competition increases for ever-scarce dollars, companies are looking to tune up their operations to give them an edge in creating a better mousetrap.

If your choice is to proceed with an job change, it needs to be well thought out and pursued with a strategy to make you look as valuable as possible to your prospective employer. Your best chance of guaranteed income improvement is in your initial negotiations.

Interview Preparation

Presenting a clear image to your potential employer of the value that you could bring to them and illustrating why you would be worth every dollar you are asking for is essential. It's a terrible strategy to go into an interview focused solely on defense and prepared to get shaken down. I don't think it's a bad idea, but I strongly believe it's more important to go in offensively with an intention of displaying what you want them to see, then proactively steering the focus in that direction. That way you'll have a far greater chance of shedding a favorable light on what you have to offer, which typically makes things go much better.

Meet Their Needs

If you are looking to move up with your job change, think of how you can add value and meet that company's needs. Review the Seven Human Needs mentioned earlier and make a list of the things you need to articulate during the interview that will clearly show how hiring you will meet both your interviewer's and the company's needs. Your goal is not necessarily to openly say, "Here is how I can meet your needs." You just need to lay out what you can or will do for them (that you know will meet their needs) and let them interpret the benefits. The simple fact that you have already practiced this exercise in your head beforehand will make it more likely that you will hit on relevant, high-impact topics. Take the following two things into consideration.

Aim High

Aim high and make your best case. Don't be afraid to push the limits of what you know and use your poker face to raise the bet, but be prepared for your bet to be called. Bluffing a little and keeping the risk and consequences in mind can give you a chance to break through some barriers. Just remember this warning: if you come up short, you may have walked away from a secure job. Only *you* know your level of skill and competence, so you have to analyze the risk versus the potential reward and make the decision.

Losing Security

This leads us to my second point, a warning. You need to consider the potential security you are giving up by moving away from the known. But honestly, I hate to see people get overly risk adverse and stuck living in what they know. Especially in today's job market, since there is potentially more risk in not chancing it.

PART TWO: TWELVE MONTH REBALANCE

Remember, this is a warning about the risk involved in this plan. I'm shining light on the opposite side of the coin, so if you have tenure in your career, a good bond with your boss, good friends you are working with, or some other non-monetary reason to stay then you may have more to consider than just the prospective in increased income.

Career Change

It would be great if everyone could choose their ideal career at a young age, pursue training, and maximize their potential in the industry of their dreams. Unfortunately, such is rarely the case.

So how in the heck can we predict where we will want to be twenty years down the road at an early age? One of the best ways is to rule out where you *don't* want to be. First, set an income goal (which will eliminate a lot of dead-end and limiting career paths). Next, make sure your career goal is in line with your personal nature and values.

Nature

This is a critical aspect in finding a fulfilling career. The last thing you want to do is focus solely on a money target only to reach that goal and find your very sociable self, for example, staring at a computer screen in a cubicle for twelve hours a day. Money will not buy you back all those hours of misery and lost enjoyment you could've gotten from a career that allowed for more human interaction.

Keep in mind though, there will probably be times on the move up the ladder when you'll have to do your time *temporarily* in environments that are less than a perfect match for your personality—after all, life is not perfect.

Luckily, scenarios and skills that come naturally to us are usually apparent long before we reach the point of needing to make a choice on our career path. Putting focus in an area that has the income potential you need and does not oppose your nature will naturally give you a much greater chance for success.

Values

Another critical area that needs to be taken into consideration is your values. You want to make sure your career goals do not conflict with the things you believe to be important. Doing so is not only crucial, but picking a career that's in line with your values can actually create a flow that will naturally help you reach your goals more easily.

CAREER FAST-TRACKING
Meeting Your Needs

Any fulfilling career will help meet most of your needs. This is important, so let it soak in. *Any fulfilling career will help meet most of your needs.*

The problem most people have is the inability to visualize (and consequently prioritize) the value of their needs. I personally hope you will take a leap of faith for the purpose of this program and evaluate how your career choice may or may not meet your needs. Hopefully a little faith in what I'm saying will mean you don't have to spend years of your life searching for the answers to why your career is so unfulfilling.

If you have reached the conclusion that your current path is not the one for you and you need to make a change, congratulations! In these situations it's always the sooner the better. You should explore all the career options that will meet your income goals, compliment your nature, not conflict with your values or beliefs, and will substantially meet all your needs. Don't limit yourself to the fields involving only the experience, skills, and knowledge that you already have. Keep your mind open to finding the ultimate fit and then determine how to get there using the strategies and information provided in this book.

With some cost versus time analysis, you may be able to make a more dramatic change than you think possible and still come out ahead. After all, a life not fully lived and filled with compromise will never be a fulfilling life.

Immediate Career Income Growth Plan

You are going to create a plan for growing your career income by listing the actions you will take within the next twelve months. Your plan may not involve any actual increase in income during this period—in fact, it may actually result in a reduction. But these actions will immediately put you on the shortest path to a career that has the potential to substantially match your personality while meeting your financial needs. If you already earn a great income but your career is unfulfilling, your plan will primarily aim for growth in life balance and satisfaction (which is absolutely ok). Remember, true wealth is not a dollar amount. It's a state of being.

Work through the following few pages to evaluate different careers and determine which one is right for you. Start by entering your ideal annual income you have previously determined or your adjusted compromise goal.

My Ideal Annual Income (page 91)	$ _____

"Money does not create a great life, it will only compliment one."
- Daniel Hartjoy

PART TWO: TWELVE MONTH REBALANCE

Meeting My Needs

What will it take for you to fulfill each of your human needs through your career? Write a brief description of the environment, people, and activities you need to best achieve this goal.

Sustenance

In order for me to feel I can be assured of my ability to sustain my lifestyle with my career, I would need:

_____
_____
_____

Connection

To feel connected and dedicated to my career and the people I work with, I would need:

_____
_____
_____

Security

To feel totally secure, have no doubts about my ability to maintain income stability, and know that I will be treated with respect in my career, I would need:

_____
_____
_____

Growth

To feel like I am continually advancing and growing in my career, I would need:

_____
_____
_____

CAREER FAST-TRACKING

Significance

For me to feel significant and like I am a valuable contributor to my career, I would need:

_____
_____
_____

Esteem

To feel I am engaged in a career that gives me pride and supports my feelings of esteem and self-esteem, I would need:

_____
_____
_____

Inner Peace

For me to feel enthusiastic and at peace in my career, aside from fulfilling my other needs I would need:

_____
_____
_____

NOTES:

_____
_____
_____
_____
_____
_____

PART TWO: TWELVE MONTH REBALANCE

Natural Match

One of the most common mistakes people make in choosing a career is not considering their personal nature. Take a few minutes to describe your ideal career situation regarding the following elements (specifically, as they relate to your nature—your *essential* characteristics and qualities).

Social Environment

What would be your ideal social environment (where you feel the most comfortable and could perform the best)?

_____
_____
_____

Pressure

Some careers are really intense while others are more laid back. Some people like challenging environments, perform well under pressure that would crack others, and would get bored if not constantly challenged. Where are you? How much pressure is comfortable for you?

_____
_____
_____

Environment

Are you someone that feels at home in a static office environment? Would you prefer to travel or be outdoors? Do you need to be busy all the time? Would you like to be part of the support staff for a key player in the organization, or do you prefer to be the key figure? Do you like board meetings, beaches, or both? What are some key environment-related aspects (physical, mental, etc.) you desire in a career?

_____
_____
_____

CAREER FAST-TRACKING
Ethics

What moral and ethical boundaries do you need to take into consideration? A vegetarian would not fit in working at a slaughter house. If you cannot tell a lie, don't get a job selling used cars. What are the moral and ethical boundaries that are deal makers and breakers for you?

_____
_____
_____

NOTES :

PART TWO: TWELVE MONTH REBALANCE

Career Assets

You likely already have some job or business experience under your belt as well as some applicable skills, abilities, and certifications. These things are what I call your current career assets. They may have significant value, so you should try to leverage them the best you can. Hopefully they will even be applicable in your ultimate career, helping you obtain the best possible starting position. Your ultimate career may not require a field change that jeopardizes the value of these assets, but if it does give serious consideration to where and how they still might be used to create value.

Make a list of your current career assets. This could include years of experience performing certain tasks or in a certain field as well as degrees, certifications, innate abilities, personality traits, relationships, associations, and so on. Think broadly about anything that you have that might be of value as an employee or in a business situation (depending on the direction you choose). These may not all be resume items, but they surely need to be leveraged as much as possible.

My Career Assets

1. _____
2. _____
3. _____
4. _____
5. _____
6. _____
7. _____
8. _____
9. _____
10. _____

CAREER FAST-TRACKING
Potential Career Paths

With all those things in mind brainstorm, research, solicit ideas from your acquaintances, and do wherever you can to come up with a list of potential careers that best fit the following four elements.

1) Meets your income goals
2) Fulfills all (or at least most) of your Seven Human Needs
3) Does not drastically conflict with your values, beliefs and/or nature
4) Makes the best use of your current career assets

Maybe you know exactly what you want to do. The list doesn't need to be fully populated. On the other hand, if you are not totally set then take some time and explore all your options. Remember, you will be spending a lot of your time and energy in your career so choose wisely.

Career Options

1. _____
2. _____
3. _____
4. _____
5. _____
6. _____
7. _____
8. _____
9. _____
10. _____

PART TWO: TWELVE MONTH REBALANCE

Decide

Now that you have done your research and taken a full inventory of the related information, you need to make a decision. This is a major choice, and you need to think it through carefully. If you want to continue the program further while this information simmers a little bit, skip to the housing section now and come back later.

If you are clear on your verdict, put your decision in ink and follow the next few exercises. Admittedly, your career choice may just be to stay where you are and take actions to excel up the ladder. If that's the case just fill in your current career and then the ideal position and pay as your goals.

My Career Goals

Industry: _____

Position: _____

Income: $ _____

Congratulations!

Whether you chose to just move up or change fields all together to something that better suits your needs and personality, I want to congratulate you on making the first big step. I mean it whole-heartedly. I have been in the same position as you and it took a big change and a lot of commitment to get out of it. Was it worth it? Absolutely, without question! This career change plan is also a great remedy for slowing hair loss and stabilizing your hair color—I can vouch for that. Best wishes moving forward!

NOTES :

_____
_____
_____
_____
_____

CAREER ACTION PLAN

Now that you have made a decision, you need to make an action plan to quickly and successfully proceed to the next level. Make a list of all the key requirements you need to meet to make this change successful. It may include getting a student loan or cutting costs as your income goes down while you are retraining. Don't worry about the "how" yet, just the "what." If you need more space just write them on a separate sheet of paper. Also, don't worry about how long your list gets. I'm going to show you a powerful method for getting results, so many of the things on your list may happen by default.

Key Requirements for Transition

1. _____
2. _____
3. _____
4. _____
5. _____
6. _____
7. _____
8. _____
9. _____
10. _____
11. _____
12. _____
13. _____
14. _____
15. _____

PART TWO: TWELVE MONTH REBALANCE

Before you go any further write down your feelings about the change you are making. Here are a couple of prompts to guide your writing. And remember, there is a point to every exercise you are given.

What enjoyment and benefits will you receive from making this change? What will your life look like five years from now?

_____
_____
_____
_____

What negative effects and pains will come from *not* making this change? If you don't make this change, what will your life look like five years from now?

_____
_____
_____
_____

Use the following Action Tree method to prioritize and track the key requirements you need to make this change happen. It's a fast and powerful method for making change. Feel free to make as many copies as you need of this form. You may also want to use it to break some key actions down into smaller steps. You can download additional electronic copies at www.WealthBuilderLifestyle.com/tools for free.

Action Tree

The Action Tree is about taking effective action and creating exceptional results with minimal effort. This is a ten-step method based on the 80/20 rule (also called Pareto's Principle) which essentially states that 20% of the effort you make will create 80% of the results. Therefore you can get a four-to-one return by focusing on the 20% that has the potential to make the largest impact first.

A tree is a great metaphor for creating something amazing from virtually nothing. If the right actions are taken with a particular seed (idea), something almost inconceivable can

CAREER ACTION PLAN

grow. On the other hand, leave that seed untouched in the wrong environment and it will remain nothing more than a seed.

For each of these steps write down the most powerful actions you can take that will generate the most results. There may only be a few for each step but think it through and try to come up with ten for each. Then go through your list and take the most powerful of those to use in the Action Tree.

Step 1: Plant the Seed

This is the most powerful step because it will take your decision and set it in motion. Make your decision a true commitment by taking action—for example, register your domain name, get a loan, update your resume and send it out to five places, sign a contract, or get some advanced training. This should be something that will create tangible results and firmly commit you to following through. This action should not be easy to change or undo.

1. _____   5. _____
2. _____   6. _____
3. _____   7. _____
4. _____   8. _____
9. _____   10. _____

Step 2: Set the Roots

This should include two power actions that will reinforce your commitment and make sure that you are going to follow through in achieving your goal. They may include getting others involved, giving notice at your job, leasing a building, or something else that makes it harder for you to break your commitment to your goal. **WARNING:** I'm not advising you to do foolish or crazy things (like quit your job) without preparation! Your actions need to make sense and be well thought out.

1. _____   5. _____
2. _____   6. _____
3. _____   7. _____
4. _____   8. _____
9. _____   10. _____

PART TWO: TWELVE MONTH REBALANCE
Step 3: Accelerate Growth

Per the tree metaphor, this step involves fertilizing the soil. This includes taking two more power actions that create a "big splash" in results, essentially hitting turbo mode on your plan to create momentum. These results should greatly accelerate your forward progress towards your goal. Things don't have to be perfect yet.

1. _____ 5. _____

2. _____ 6. _____

3. _____ 7. _____

4. _____ 8. _____

9. _____ 10. _____

Step 4: Shape Your Results

You've taken massive action and created major results with big hits, and now you need to take some powerful steps towards filling in the voids. What do you need to do to support your big changes? Maybe you need to do a little damage control to get things inline. Maybe you have dedicated all your time and energy into accelerating your education and now it's time to get your outer image in shape. Maybe some new clothes and a makeover are in order to align your newfound inner strength with your outer appearance. Whatever it may be, this should help balance your massive growth initiated in Step Three.

1. _____ 5. _____

2. _____ 6. _____

3. _____ 7. _____

4. _____ 8. _____

9. _____ 10. _____

CAREER ACTION PLAN

Step 5: Perfect Your Outcome

These final actions are going to help clean up the mess and polish off your achievement. When you trim a tree you make it look great, but it makes a big mess. It may be perfect, but other areas may need to be put back in shape for you to feel the full value of the change. What power actions can you take to polish off the little details so your new goals can become a lasting part of your new life?

1. _____
2. _____
3. _____
4. _____
9. _____

5. _____
6. _____
7. _____
8. _____
10. _____

Conclusion

Remember, I said the most powerful 20% of your efforts can create 80% of your results. Keep the broad picture in mind, always focusing on the most powerful 20% that will get you the most results in achieving your goals. Half of what we tend to think we need to do doesn't really need to be done.

NOTES :

_____
_____
_____
_____
_____
_____
_____
_____

PART TWO: TWELVE MONTH REBALANCE

Use the following form to plan, track, and monitor progress on your goal.

Career Goal Action Tree

Goal _____

STEP	Progress Tracker — shade one box for every action completed	☐ ☐ ☐ ☐ ☐ ☐ ☐ ☐
	Plant the Seed – Write one action that will turn an idea into a real decision.	
1	Your Seed Action	_____ ☐
	Set the Roots – Take two power actions that will further commit you to your goal.	
2	First Influential, Root-Setting Action	1. _____ ☐
	Second Influential, Root-Setting Action	2. _____ ☐
	Accelerate Growth – Take two more power actions that will produce massive growth.	
3	First Influential Fertilization Action	1. _____ ☐
	Second Influential Fertilization Action	2. _____ ☐
	Shape Your Results – Take two more power actions to fill voids and refine your approach.	
4	First Influential Shaping Action	1. _____ ☐
	Second Influential Shaping Action	2. _____ ☐
	Perfect Your Outcome – Take two more power actions that clean up any remaining mess.	
5	First Influential Clean-Up Action	1. _____ ☐
	Second Influential Clean-Up Action	2. _____ ☐

Check the appropriate box after each action is completed.

HOUSING

Typically one of our biggest expenses (if not the biggest) is our home, whether rented or purchased. I saved this part for after the other easy adjustments to your spending because it will likely take months or even the entire year to bring this in line.

    Start by entering the current amount you spend and the guideline amount you are trying to get your housing cost in line with below. If your current housing expenses are within the guideline amount, congratulations! Feel free to skip the rest of this section, although you may still want to read through it just to understand the concept in case you may be able to apply this philosophy in other areas or at another time.

Current Housing Expenses (pg 68)	$ _____
Guideline Housing Expenses (pg 68)	$ _____
Housing Cost Reduction Necessary (current expenses – guideline expenses)	$ _____

NOTES :

_____
_____
_____
_____
_____
_____
_____
_____
_____
_____

PART TWO: TWELVE MONTH REBALANCE

Renting

If you are currently a renter there are two initial options for getting your numbers inline. First, you could evaluate a potential move to a less expensive rental arrangement. This would be the easiest method mathematically, but may not be possible based on the region you live in. Second, you could buy a home that fits within your budget.

Option One: Relocate

Our goal is to get your costs down without dramatically impacting your quality of life. I'm not advising you to do something like move into an unsafe area with poor schools to save a buck (as the real consequences of doing something like are not worth it). On the other hand, doing an honest evaluation may open up some better options. Maybe you could consider a different location, a smaller unit, or a building with fewer luxurious amenities. Do some market research and enter the rental cost for any potential rental option that would be less than what you are currently paying.

Current Rental Cost	$ _____
New Rental Cost	$ _____
Monthly Amount Saved by Moving (current rent – new rent)	$ _____

We are not going to factor in the moving costs because the goal is to get you in balance within twelve months and that would be a one-time expense. It may be a minor setback, but if you get in balance the cost will be offset by your wealth building progress in the near future.

NOTES :

_____
_____
_____
_____
_____
_____

HOUSING
Pros of Option One

Enter the five advantages you would benefit from by making this move. When considering your new location take into account the schools, your location of work, and other places you will frequent like stores, parks, and recreational options. Considering these factors can help reduce your costs in other areas and make the change more appealing. Would it positively affect any of your relationships with friends or family? When you consider your relationship consequences, consider the possibility of maybe breaking or weakening some ties with people in your life that aren't really contributing in a positive way. You may also be able to move closer to some that are positive influences on you.

1. _____
2. _____
3. _____
4. _____
5. _____

Cons of Option One

Enter the five likely disadvantages that would come from making this move. Remember to consider all of the things we did for the benefits list above. How would this adversely impact your quality of life?

1. _____
2. _____
3. _____
4. _____
5. _____

Is the relocating option a viable way to get you in balance or at least substantially closer without destroying your quality of life? Remember, this is a short-term fix on the way to a richer and more fulfilling life. A little sacrifice in the short term can greatly accelerate your advancement towards a better future.

PART TWO: TWELVE MONTH REBALANCE
Option Two: Buy a Home

Look at purchasing a home rather than renting. As I write this, home loan interest rates are extremely low and housing costs are down due to the economic slowdown. This may very well be one of the best times to enter the housing market for years to come. Sure, the economy may be slow for some time but rental costs are not likely to decline much (if any), so buying a place at or near the same cost as renting could be your best bet.

Do a little research and fill in the boxes below to see if you could meet your housing cost reduction by purchasing a home. If it will cost you more than what you are currently paying, enter the Monthly Cost Difference as a negative (so you at least know the difference).

Current Housing Cost	$ _____
New Home Cost	$ _____
Monthly Cost Difference (current housing − new home cost)	$ _____

This may not be a feasible option at the moment but even if the cost of purchasing will be more expensive than renting do this exercise and finish your research.

Pros of Option Two

Enter the five advantages you would benefit from by making this move. When considering your new location take into account the schools, your location of work, and other places you need to travel to like stores, parks, and recreational options. Taking these factors into account can help reduce your costs in other areas and make the change more appealing. Also, would it positively affect any of your relationships with friends or family? When you consider your relationship consequences, consider the possibility of maybe breaking or weakening some ties with people in your life that aren't really contributing in a positive way. You may also be able to move closer to some that are beneficial to you.

1. _____
2. _____
3. _____
4. _____
5. _____

HOUSING

Cons of Option Two

Enter the five likely disadvantages that would come from making this move. Remember to consider all of the things you did for the benefits list. How would this adversely impact your quality of life?

1. _____
2. _____
3. _____
4. _____
5. _____

    Is Option Two a viable way to get you substantially closer to being in balance without totally destroying your quality of life?

Home Buying

We are going to look into a number of home buying options that will allow you to get closer to (if not fully) in balance with your guideline. One of the great things about owning (or at least being in control of) a home is that you can use your house any way you like, potentially even in a way that can create additional income. We'll be examining four different options.

Option One: Refinance

Is there a refinancing option that can help get your numbers in line with your goals? Research your options online and talk to a mortgage broker to find out how much you could reduce your monthly costs via refinancing and what the total transaction cost would be.

    Do not make the mistake of doing a singular evaluation—just a lower payment—which your lender will likely have you focus on. Extending your loan at a lower interest rate can often times lower your monthly payment, but may increase the overall cost you will pay for your home—thus making it a bad financial decision.

NOTES :

_____

_____

PART TWO: TWELVE MONTH REBALANCE

Use the following simple worksheet to evaluate your refinancing options. Determine if there is one that will provide you with a solution that makes your home more affordable today without increasing your overall cost. Fill in the boxes and complete the formulas to see how different options really compare. Not only will this help you compare assorted loan options, but it will also give you an idea of how much you're really going to end up paying for your home (which is much different than the purchase price most people focus on). You will need to go online and use an amortization calculator or talk to a mortgage broker to complete this step.

Option One Analysis				
Item or Calculation	Current Mortgage	Option One	Option Two	Option Three
Loan Balance	$_____	$_____	$_____	$_____
Fees Added to Loan	N/A	$_____	$_____	$_____
Total Loan Amount	$_____	$_____	$_____	$_____
New Payment	N/A	$_____	$_____	$_____
Determine the monthly cost to pay off your refinancing fees in twelve months.				
One-time Fees	N/A	$_____	$_____	$_____
One-time Fees ÷ 12	N/A	$_____	$_____	$_____
		+	+	+
New Payment	N/A	$_____	$_____	$_____
Ongoing Payment (new or existing)	$_____	$_____	$_____	$_____
Enter new and existing interest rates to see the real cost versus interest rate difference.				
Interest Rate (APR)	_____%	_____%	_____%	_____%

NOTES:

_____

_____

_____

HOUSING

On the next table, multiply the total number of loan payments required to pay off the loan times the payment amount. This will determine the total of all your payments, which will give you a better idea of what each option will cost long term. Remember to use only the months left when calculating your existing loan amount.

Option One Analysis (Cont.)				
Loan Length	_____ × 12 =	_____ × 12 =	_____ × 12 =	_____ × 12 =
Months to Pay Off Loan	_____ ×	_____ ×	_____ ×	_____ ×
Ongoing Payment (from previous form)	$_____ =	$_____ =	$_____ =	$_____ =
Total of All Payments	$_____	$_____	$_____	$_____
This is the **real total cost** of your refinance options. Add the total of all your payments to any one-time fees that will not be rolled in to your new loan.				
Total of All Payments + One-Time Fees	$_____	$_____	$_____	$_____

The most important numbers you will want to look at in the last two worksheets are in the shaded boxes, and the darkest box is ultimately the most important. You should still look over the other boxes to get a feel for how different interest rates and loan lengths can affect your payments and the total amount you will need to pay. You will want to make sure that if you do have to pay some loan fees you will be able to cover the additional amount to get them paid off during the Twelve-Month Rebalance. Otherwise, the new payment amount may be deceptive and not actually the best way to help you get in balance. If you roll the payments into your loan you will want to look at the overall impact on the total you will pay for your home.

Although I advise people to pay off their loans in fifteen years or less, I typically recommend they get a thirty-year mortgage. With that in mind, if you have for example seventeen years left on your existing mortgage I would never advise you to take out a new thirty-year loan to make it more affordable. It may still make sense to refinance to a twenty-year loan if the interest rate is lower and the total loan costs are equal to or less than your current loan. Unfortunately, banks will not typically be interested in loans of a random length and a fifteen-year loan may not do enough to make your payments work out (even with a lower interest rate).

PART TWO: TWELVE MONTH REBALANCE
Option Two: Sell Your Existing Home

I know this may be a sad option to even consider, but if you're not currently building wealth at a rate that's in line with the Wealth Builder Lifestyle, it could very well be necessary. If you're substantially outside of the guidelines because your mortgage is eating you alive, you may need to consider selling your home and downsizing. This can lead to having a home paid off much quicker. Then you can upgrade to a more expensive home later as your wealth increases and you can afford to do it while maintaining positive wealth creation.

In the following worksheet you will see a few examples based on different hypothetical scenarios regarding downsizing. These three scenarios, although hypothetical, are 100% possible and only require varying actions. They assume a starting home value of $300,000 with $71,600 in equity, meaning the payoff balance of the loan is $228,400. The amazing thing about the two wealth builder options is they both assume an initial equity loss of $31,500. Even with that initial loss, by the end of the 18-year period covered your wealth would be over $55,000 higher and it wouldn't cost you one penny more.

Sadly, most people stay locked into the "no change" scenario due to a lack of financial education, laziness, or an unwillingness to live a little more humbly. The result of that thinking is that over 18 years they will spend $328,320 to gain $228,400 in wealth, not even breaking even with the value of their investment contribution.

NOTES :
_____
_____
_____
_____
_____
_____
_____
_____
_____
_____

HOUSING

In all fairness, I have included no real estate appreciation (which you could expect to add to your total investment value). I left out appreciation for simplicity and because it can vary greatly. I prefer to look at your home as a security investment that you don't expect to make a huge return on but rather hope to see consistent positive growth in value while striving for complete ownership as quickly as possible.

Option Two Example			
(Example based on 4.5% APR)			
Existing Home		New Home	
Likely Sale Amount (market value)	$300,000	Purchase Price	$210,000
Sale Cost (realtor and closing costs)	$24,000	Buyer's Fees (closing cost)	$7,500
Existing Loan Payoff	$228,400	Down Payment (proceeds from home sale)	$47,600
Net Proceeds From Sale (sale amount – sale cost – loan payoff)	$47,600	New Loan Amount	$169,900
Equity (sale amount – loan balance)	$71,600	Equity (purchase price – loan balance)	$40,100
Monthly Mortgage Payment	$1,520	Monthly Mortgage Payment	$1,149
×		×	
Remaining Loan Length (in months)	216	Loan Length (in months)	216
=		=	
Total of Remaining Payments	$328,320	Total of Remaining Payments	$248,184

In the previous example you initially lose $31,500 in equity which appears to be a step backwards. Looking down the road to the time when your existing home is paid off you will see that you will have spent $328,320 dollars to have a $300,000 asset (no inflation accounted for). On your new home, you will have paid $248,184 to own your $210,000 asset. In this way, it still would appear more sensible to keep your existing home and just suck up the larger payments. That is, until you apply the following Wealth Builder Lifestyle strategies.

We are going to compare two alternatives to the option of doing nothing. For the first, we will invest the difference between the two loan options into something with an anticipated 10% return for the full loan length of 216 months. For the second, we will follow an accelerated payoff plan (paying the current monthly mortgage payment of $1,520 instead of the new $1,149 payment to pay the loan off quicker) and then invest for the last 71 months. The total amount paid over the 18-year period (216 months) is the same for all three

PART TWO: TWELVE MONTH REBALANCE

of these options. The only thing that changes is the method of spending which is made possible by downsizing into a more affordable home that will allow a small contribution to a Wealth Builder Lifestyle. The total investment in each scenario is 216 × $1,520 for a grand total of $328,320.

Option Two Example (cont.)			
(Investments based on 10% return)			
Investing the Difference		**Accelerated Payoff Then Invest**	
Total Monthly Investment	$371	Monthly Mortgage Payment	$1,520
Contribution Length (in months)	216	Loan Length (months)	145
Total Pre-Interest Investment	$80,136	Total of Remaining Payments	$220,400
Total Investment Value at 10%	$213,844	Accelerated Payoff Savings	$27,784
		Monthly Investment	$1,520
		Investment Length (in months)	71
		Total Pre-Interest Investment	$107,920
		Total Investment Value at 10%	$145,552
Wealth Impact After 18 Years			
Current Home (no change)			$300,000
New Home (Investing the Difference)			$423,844
New Home (Accelerated Payoff Plus Investment)			$355,552

Option Two Analysis

Use the following form to enter your actual information and evaluate the downsizing concept. One other thing to consider when doing this evaluation is that I used the purchase price as the new home value in the examples. There are currently many foreclosures and distressed properties on the market, so if you did your due diligence you could likely purchase your new home well below its current market value. This could give you the potential to improve your equity position rather than take a loss like the example shows.

NOTES :

_____
_____
_____
_____

HOUSING

Option Two Analysis

Existing Home		New Home	
Likely Sale Amount (market value)	$_____	Purchase Price	$_____
Sale Cost (realtor and closing costs)	$_____	Buyer's Fees (closing cost)	$_____
Existing Loan Payoff	$_____	Down Payment (proceeds from home sale)	$_____
Net Proceeds From Sale (sale – sale cost – loan payoff)	$_____	**New Loan Amount**	$_____
Equity (sale amount – loan balance)	$_____	Equity (purchase price – loan balance)	$_____
Monthly Mortgage Payment	$_____	Monthly Mortgage Payment	$_____
×		×	
Remaining Loan Length (in months)	$_____	Loan Length (in months)	$_____
=		=	
Total of Remaining Payments	$_____	**Total of Remaining Payments**	$_____

Use online interest and amortization calculators for the following form.

Investing the Difference		Accelerated Payoff Then Invest	
Total Monthly Investment	$_____	Monthly Mortgage Payment	$_____
Contribution Length (months)	$_____	Loan Length (months)	$_____
Total Pre-Interest Investment	$_____	**Total of Remaining Payments**	$_____
Total Investment Value	$_____	**Accelerated Payoff Savings**	$_____
		Monthly Investment	$_____
		Investment Length (in months)	$_____
		Total Pre-Interest Investment	$_____
		Total Investment Value	$_____

Wealth Impact After _____ Years	
Current Home (no change)	$_____
New Home (Investing the Difference)	$_____
New Home (Accelerated Payoff Plus Investment)	$_____

PART TWO: TWELVE MONTH REBALANCE
Option Three: Buy an Additional Home

Buy another, less expensive home. If you have a larger home than you can currently afford but don't want to or can't sell it, consider this option. Rent your existing home out and either buy another more affordable one or just rent a cheaper home temporarily. Sounds crazy, right? If you have a great, beautiful home why would you want to move out and rent something else? If you can't afford it but the numbers work, you can still keep your dream home. Maybe in three to five years your income will increase enough to make that home payment suitable for a Wealth Builder Lifestyle. The benefit of renting another place for yourself is that you are not locked into another loan and can move out at the end of your lease. The long-term drawback, of course, is that the rent is likely to continue going up.

On the other hand, if you choose to buy another home you are locked into a payment at today's price and over the next few years as your income increases the payments will get easier to make. You will still maintain your interest write-offs and even gain some others.

Another benefit of buying an additional house is that you will be building equity in two homes while only paying for one. The principle paid down on both houses and any appreciation will continue to add to your wealth. So not only will you reduce your housing costs, but you will actually have renters buying a home for you as well. Essentially you'll be using the bank's money to build wealth.

Depending on home values and rental rates in your area, this may or may not be a good option for you. Your credit and current interest rates will also affect the feasibility of this method of wealth creation. The results from living a more humble standard of living in the short term can lead to a much richer future in the long term.

NOTES:

_____

_____

_____

_____

_____

_____

_____

HOUSING
Option Three Analysis

The following two forms are valuable tools that you can use to evaluate purchasing another less expensive home to live in while renting out your current home.

Do a little market research for your area and input the answers below. You don't have to go to extreme lengths initially, just try to get your estimates close. If this approach looks like it will work out and make sense for you, then you can tighten up the numbers. You will also need an amortization calculator which can be found online to determine your approximate new mortgage payment.

Option Three Analysis	
Existing Home	**Potential Second Home**
Potential Monthly Rent $_____	Existing Mortgage Payment $_____
Potential Monthly Rent × 11 = $_____	New Mortgage Payment - $_____
(allows 8% for vacancy) ÷ 12 =	=
Monthly Rental Income $_____	**Monthly Amount Saved** $_____
Monthly Mortgage Payment $_____	One-Time Cost (down payment and other) $_____
Other Expenses Not Covered by Renters $_____	
Combine all expenses	Equity (house value − new loan amount) - $_____
	=
Combined Monthly Expenses $_____	Amount Lost by Purchase (will likely be negative) $_____
Subtract Monthly Expenses from Rent Income	Recovery Cost ÷ 12 = $_____
Approximate Monthly Net (gain or loss) $_____	**New Mortgage Payment + Recovery Cost** $_____

PART TWO: TWELVE MONTH REBALANCE

It is likely that you will have some uncovered purchase costs that are not offset by equity. Ideally, we would like to get these paid off with savings within the first year. Unfortunately, it may not be possible to completely pay off all these costs within the first twelve months. For simplicity in this analysis we will figure out the uncovered balance and compare it against any future gains.

There are numerous ways to evaluate the cost of dealing with the remaining balance. You will have to do the math and evaluate how quickly to pay down any carryover balance. It may make sense to just continue paying steadily after the first year until it's fully paid off by deferring investments or reducing the original amount being paid and investing the difference.

A word of caution: if you defer paying off the carryover, give careful consideration to the lack of financial flexibility this will cause. Extending the length of time you will be carrying additional debt payments will limit your ability to easily reduce your overhead should you fall into hard financial times. You can easily suspend your investment contributions during a hard time, so knocking out your remaining purchase expenses before investing may have some merit.

With the addition of your new home you will be gaining equity in two properties while reducing monthly expenses which will allow you to build some investment wealth. Use the following form to calculate your potential wealth creation.

Option Three Potential Wealth Creation	
Existing Mortgage Payment $_____ − New Mortgage Payment + Recovery Cost $_____ (previous page) =	Existing Mortgage Payment $_____ − New Mortgage Payment $_____ =
Monthly Net $_____	**Mortgage Monthly Net** $_____
× 12 =	+ Approximate Monthly Net $_____ (from previous chart) =
Total Uncovered Expenses (after 1st year) $_____	**Total Available to Invest** (after 1st year) $_____

HOUSING

On the following form, use an online amortization calculator and your loan terms to determine your Real Estate Equity wealth creation potential over time (top half). For each corresponding time period, add the investment wealth created during that same time period (lower left) to the real estate equity gains (top half) and enter the totals in the lower right.

Use an online compound interest calculator to determine your investment wealth creation possibility over time. Use the Total Available to Invest as your monthly contribution amount. Subtract the Total Uncovered Expenses from your calculations to determine the true wealth created. In addition, exclude twelve months from all investment calculations as that money has already been used to offset the money lost during the purchase.

Option Three Wealth Increase			
Real Estate Equity Gains			
Term	Existing	New	Combined
5 Years (60 months)	$_____	$_____	$_____
10 Years (120 months)	$_____	$_____	$_____
20 Years (240 months)	$_____	$_____	$_____
30 Years (360 months)	$_____	$_____	$_____

Investment Wealth Gains	Value	Time	Existing	New + Inv.	Combined
5 Year (based on only 4 years)	$_____	5 Years	$_____	$_____	$_____
10 Year (based on only 9 years)	$_____	10 Years	$_____	$_____	$_____
20 Year (based on only 19 years)	$_____	20 Years	$_____	$_____	$_____
30 Year (based on only 29 years)	$_____	30 Years	$_____	$_____	$_____

Enter the amounts from your New [Asset Equity] + Inv. [Investment] inputs above into the chart below in order to create a summary of your potential wealth creation over time.

Wealth Increase Summary for New Strategy			
5 Years $_____	10 Years $_____	20 Years $_____	30 Years $_____

PART TWO: TWELVE MONTH REBALANCE

It's always important to give serious consideration before taking on any additional debt. Although this can be a great method of leveraging other people's money (OPM) and building wealth, it can also create added financial risk.

Some things you should consider are how secure your job is, if you have an adequate amount of money set aside in the event of a setback, and if the long-term benefits make the risk worth it. The majority of people will successfully build wealth when using this method, but it should not be jumped into carelessly.

Option Four: Employing Your Home

Use your home to generate money. If you're willing to be open-minded and consider all your options, you may have income opportunities available to you that you are not currently capitalizing on.

Renting out a spare bedroom may bring in the few hundred dollars needed to get you inline. Remember, the most powerful principles in this program are not based on making big, one-time hits but rather consistent little ones that add up to be substantial over time. You may not want to give up your privacy for a few hundred dollars a month, and I get that, but this may be one of the easiest ways to initially get in balance and start building wealth.

There are a lot of students and single individuals out there that just need an affordable place to call home. I know many people that have rented to foreign exchange students, elderly folks, and other good people that just need a chance. If you have land or perhaps a detached garage you don't necessarily use, you may opt to rent out a portion of it for someone to store a boat or RV.

If you haven't thought through how you could have your assets building wealth for you, I would highly recommend looking into it. In the last 20 years or so opportunity and money have come pretty easily. As we move into the future and things tighten up, we need to explore all our opportunities, capitalize on them when we can, and increase our financial security.

HOUSING

Make a list of the potential options for using your home to generate additional income. One thing to take into consideration is that just like any rental home there may be times of vacancy, so use an amount that safely takes that into consideration.

Home Income Generation	
Potential Income-Generating Option	Potential Monthly Income
1. _____	$ _____
2. _____	$ _____
3. _____	$ _____
4. _____	$ _____
5. _____	$ _____
Total Potential Additional Income	$ _____

I would never advise someone to try to make a "perfect" plan. No matter how hard you try, you will likely find it still has flaws. Worse yet, spending too much time focusing on the planning phase may cause you to lose your drive to do anything because your life is no longer fun. So just use these tools and strategies to a reasonable extent to compile your ultimate plan. The most important aspect of any successful plan is that it adequately provides constant, safe wealth creation and that it has the potential to get you to your goal.

NOTES :

_____
_____
_____
_____
_____
_____
_____

REBALANCE BLUEPRINT

Now we're going to get this abundance of information boiled down to a clear plan for transitioning to a Wealth Builder Lifestyle.

You need to create a simple image in your mind of exactly what you need to do to succeed. That image will represent a simple action plan that you will be able to follow daily with very little effort or thought, this will turn your goals into reality. You also need to have a "story" that you can articulate fluently which will serve as your wealth builder rebalance philosophy. It will represent the strategies you will be using to make your transition. The reason why you are doing this is because if you can't visualize and articulate your goals, you are far less likely to achieve them. Whether they realize it or not, everyone who achieves millionaire status has good key habits that support their wealth building lifestyle.

Security Cushion

Enter your weekly security cushion distributions in the form below. This will give you a clear snapshot of your security cushion plan for the Twelve-Month Rebalance. You can find the monthly contribution total you previously determined on page 76 and then just determine the weeks or pay periods when you will have the money available to make the contributions.

Security Cushion (Twelve-Month Rebalance)		
Weekly Contributions	Amount	Twelve Month Formula
Week One	$_____	Total Monthly Contribution
Week Two	$_____	×
Week Three	$_____	12
Week Four	$_____	=
Total Monthly Contribution $_____		Twelve-Month Goal $_____

Spending Reductions

Enter your finalized personal and necessity spending cuts in the following form. These will be your new boundaries of things not to spend on. If you are reducing your budget by one latte a day, for example, put it on the list as well as a plan for how you will achieve it. For the best

PART TWO: TWELVE MONTH REBALANCE

results, don't leave a void: if you cut a latte, replace it with a free or less expensive alternative such as walking for fifteen minutes.

Your previously determined list of cuts can be found on pages 79 and 80.

Spending Reductions (Twelve-Month Rebalance)	
Necessity Expense / Action Required	Monthly Total
1. _____ / _____	$ _____
2. _____ / _____	$ _____
3. _____ / _____	$ _____
4. _____ / _____	$ _____
5. _____ / _____	$ _____
6. _____ / _____	$ _____
7. _____ / _____	$ _____
8. _____ / _____	$ _____
9. _____ / _____	$ _____
10. _____ / _____	$ _____
Personal Expense / Action Required	Monthly Total
1. _____ / _____	$ _____
2. _____ / _____	$ _____
3. _____ / _____	$ _____
4. _____ / _____	$ _____
5. _____ / _____	$ _____
6. _____ / _____	$ _____
7. _____ / _____	$ _____
8. _____ / _____	$ _____
9. _____ / _____	$ _____
10. _____ / _____	$ _____
Combined Total of Cuts	$ _____

REBLANCE BLUEPRINT
Debt Reduction

Use the debt reduction hit list information you created from page 86 below.

Hit List (Hit Amount $ _____)						
Creditor	Loan Balance	Minimum Payment	Hit List Payment	Hit Start Date	Payoff Date	APR
_____	$_____	$_____	$_____	_____	_____	____
_____	$_____	$_____	$_____	_____	_____	____
_____	$_____	$_____	$_____	_____	_____	____
_____	$_____	$_____	$_____	_____	_____	____
_____	$_____	$_____	$_____	_____	_____	____
_____	$_____	$_____	$_____	_____	_____	____
_____	$_____	$_____	$_____	_____	_____	____
_____	$_____	$_____	$_____	_____	_____	____
_____	$_____	$_____	$_____	_____	_____	____
_____	$_____	$_____	$_____	_____	_____	____
_____	$_____	$_____	$_____	_____	_____	____
Initial Loan Total $_____			Yearend Balance $_____			

NOTES :

_____
_____
_____
_____
_____
_____
_____

PART TWO: TWELVE MONTH REBALANCE
Rebalance Investment Plan

You should have come up with an amount that you have available each month to put towards investments. Use the amount you came up with from page 83 in the next worksheet.

It's not nearly as complicated or scary to figure this stuff out as you may think. Such emotions probably exist simply because you have never done it. Wealth builders don't start out financially savvy, it's a learning process that you too can learn.

If you're not sure yet which specific investments you're going to use for each category, that's fine, just list the investment amount for each category. Then, at least track and put your investment funds into a savings account so you can get started on your rebalance right away. When you are ready, apply it towards the appropriate investment. Use the following rebalancing guidelines until you can fully meet your standard program guideline percentages.

Investment Allocations (Twelve-Month Rebalance)					
Investment Category	Total Investment Contribution		Rebalance Guideline		Category Contribution
Security		×	40%	=	$_____
Growth	$_____	×	30%	=	$_____
Business		×	30%	=	$_____

By completing these forms you will be getting more familiar with where the money's at and should be able to crosscheck all your answers (i.e. the monthly total investments above should equal your monthly total below). If you find a mistake, just go back and see where you went wrong.

Determine the week of the month that specifically corresponds to when you will be making your investment contributions. This will vary based on which pay period or week of the month the allocated amount will be available to you.

Investment Distributions (Twelve-Month Rebalance)					
Investment Category	Week One	Week Two	Week Three	Week Four	Monthly Total
Security	$_____	$_____	$_____	$_____	$_____
Growth	$_____	$_____	$_____	$_____	$_____
Business	$_____	$_____	$_____	$_____	$_____
Totals	$_____	$_____	$_____	$_____	$_____

REBLANCE BLUEPRINT
Career Fast-Tracking

Although you will use the action tree created in the career section for specific progress tracking of your goal, list the key steps below to create an overview of the actions required to make your change. For example: Step 1, apply for student loans in next 30 days; Step 2, enroll in trade school within sixty days; and Step 3, search for the best possible position in your new field of work to start building experience. Use as few or many steps as you need. Remember, this is just a broad overview.

Step 1: _____

_____

Step 2: _____

_____

Step 3: _____

_____

Step 4: _____

_____

Step 5: _____

_____

Step 6: _____

_____

Step 7: _____

_____

Step 8: _____

_____

Step 9: _____

_____

Step 10: _____

_____

PART TWO: TWELVE MONTH REBALANCE

This Action Tree will help you plan, track, and monitor progress on your goal. It should contain the same information you previously entered on page 118. If you don't want to re-fill it in here, you can cut out your original one or download and print out a separate Rebalance Blueprint to create your plan.

Career Goal Action Tree

Goal _____

STEP	Progress Tracker — shade one box for every action completed	☐ ☐ ☐ ☐ ☐ ☐ ☐ ☐ ☐
	Plant the Seed – Write one action that will turn an idea into a real decision.	
1	Your Seed Action	_____ ☐
	Set the Roots – Take two power actions that will further commit you to your goal.	
2	First Influential, Root-Setting Action	1. _____ ☐
	Second Influential, Root-Setting Action	2. _____ ☐
	Accelerate Growth – Take two more power actions that will produce massive growth.	
3	First Influential Fertilization Action	1. _____ ☐
	Second Influential Fertilization Action	2. _____ ☐
	Shape Your Results – Take two more power actions to fill voids and refine your approach.	
4	First Influential Shaping Action	1. _____ ☐
	Second Influential Shaping Action	2. _____ ☐
	Perfect Your Outcome – Take two more power actions that clean up any remaining mess.	
5	First Influential Clean-Up Action	1. _____ ☐
	Second Influential Clean-Up Action	2. _____ ☐

Check the appropriate box after each action is completed.

REBLANCE BLUEPRINT
Rebalance Housing Plan

Based on what you read earlier in the rental and housing section, what have you decided?

☐ No change ☐ Changes per the following plan

In the simplest and most direct way, describe the changes you will make. Then list the action steps you need to take (including the trigger dates or dollar amounts required for such changes). For example: Step 1, immediately start saving $200 for each of the next 6 months; Step 2, in 5 months start looking for a new apartment; and Step 3, in one year (on __/__/____) I will move to a cheaper apartment.

I will make the following change to my housing situation:

_____

_____

In order to successfully complete this change, I will take the following steps when the step trigger is reached:

Step 1: _____

Trigger: _____

Step 2: _____

Trigger: _____

Step 3: _____

Trigger: _____

Step 4: _____

Trigger: _____

Step 5: _____

Trigger: _____

PART TWO: TWELVE MONTH REBALANCE

End of Year Goals

Cutting and reducing things is never fun and goes against our need to grow. You want to realign your focus to the future pleasure that will be created by taking these actions, and one of the best ways to do that is to have a clear picture of your goals. I don't mean a physical picture (although that helps), I mean a picture in your mind that you can focus on. Essentially, I'm talking about a snapshot of the outcome you seek and the pleasure associated with it.

You need to be aware of the cuts and changes you need to make to achieve your goals, but your focus should primarily be on the positives. For example, your growing bank account, increasing investments, more security (thanks to your fully-funded cushion), and your net worth being on the rise should all be great consequences of your efforts. Take a few minutes here to visualize your end goals. You can ask yourself the following questions to help inspire your vision.

What would the home you live in look like?

What kind of cars would you drive?

What would you be doing to earn income?

How many hours a week would you work?

What would your coworkers be like?

Are you the boss or a key player?

What would your bank statement look like each month?

What toys would you have (boat, motorcycle, recreational vehicle, etc.)?

What lifestyle would you be able to provide for your kids?

How would your friends and family view you?

What would you be able to do to contribute and give back?

These are just a few examples of questions you might ask yourself to stimulate your mind's thought processes. It may be helpful to create a list of your own questions that specifically apply to you that will hopefully trigger thoughts about your most important priorities.

"It's not where you start in life that matters, it's where you end up!"

- Daniel Hartjoy

REBLANCE BLUEPRINT
Goal Vision Board

A physical image can also help you reflect on and support your mental one. Taking a little time to create a physical snapshot of your outcomes/goals can help support the burning of your goals into your conscious (and ultimately subconscious) mind. A goal vision board can be a handy tool for helping to keep you focused.

     A goal vision board is a simple collage of pictures or symbols that represent the goals you wish to achieve. To make one, pick up some type of backing such as poster or foam board which is available at any office supply or box store. It should be of a size that comfortably fits where you plan to keep it. You will want the board in a place where you will see it often. Cut out pictures, text snippets, or other symbols that represent your goals, outcomes, and desires. Attach them to your board in a collage, then every time you see it, take a moment to look it over and think about your action plan for making your goals a reality.

NOTES:

_____

_____

_____

_____

_____

_____

_____

_____

_____

_____

_____

PART TWO: TWELVE MONTH REBALANCE

Use the following form to help estimate your net wealth at the end of your twelve month rebalance. Use a compound interest calculator (such as the one available at http://www.interestcalc.org) to estimate your ending investment values.

Net Wealth Evaluator (Twelve-Month Rebalance)			
(what you own)		(what you owe)	
Liquid Assets		**Unsecured Debt**	
Security Cushion	$_____	Credit Cards	$_____
Cash, Other	$_____	Other Loans	$_____
Total Liquid Assets	$_____	Total Unsecured Debts	$_____
Real Property Assets		**Real Property Liabilities**	
Primary Residence	$_____	Primary Residence	$_____
Other Real Estate	$_____	Other Real Estate	$_____
Planes, Boats, RVs	$_____	Planes, Boats, RVs	$_____
Automobiles (incl. Motorcycles)	$_____	Automobiles (incl. motorcycles)	$_____
Personal Property	$_____	Other	$_____
Other	$_____	Other	$_____
Total Property Assets	$_____	Total Property Liabilities	$_____
Investment Assets (anticipated end values)		Total All Liabilities	$_____
		Rebalance Total Net Wealth	
Security Investments	$_____		
Growth Investments	$_____	Total (all assets)	$_____
Business Investments	$_____	Total (all liabilities)	$_____
Total Investment Assets	$_____	Net Wealth	$_____
Total All Assets	$_____	(net wealth = assets − liabilities)	

REBLANCE BLUEPRINT
Visual Progress Tracker

Use the following visual progress tracker to enter your current standings and your future goals. Shade in the progress meters as you move closer to each goal. Think of this like a goal dashboard that measures your progress towards each achievement. Following are specific instructions for each of the six categories you will be tracking.

Security Cushion – For your Goal, enter the difference between where you are now and your One-Year Goal, this is the total amount you are looking to grow your cushion by. Divide the difference by twelve and enter the Monthly Goal amount you need to contribute to reach this goal. Shade one cell for each time you save the equivalent of your monthly goal. If you save only half of it one month, for example, shade half a cell.

Spending Reduction – For your Monthly Goal, enter your current spending budget. For your Spending Reduction Goal, subtract your current spending from your Monthly Goal. Then for your One-Year Goal, multiply your Spending Reduction Goal by twelve. Shade one cell for each time you reduce your spending the equivalent of your monthly goal. If you reduce it by only half for one month, for example, shade half a cell.

Investments Goal – For your One-Year Goal, enter the investment balance you wish to have at the end of the year. For your Investments Goal, enter the difference between your current investment balance and your One-Year Goal. Then for your Monthly Goal, divide your Investment Goal by twelve. Shade one cell for each time you invest the equivalent of your monthly goal.

Debt Reduction – For your Debt Reduction Goal, enter the difference between where you are now and your One-Year Goal. Your One-Year Goal should be the ending balance from your Debt Reduction Hit List. Divide the difference by twelve and enter the amount as your Monthly Goal. Shade one cell for each time you pay off the equivalent of your Monthly Goal.

Career Income – For your Career Income Increase, subtract your Current Income from your Target Income and enter that amount. There are ten boxes, each one of which represents 10% of your career increase. If you get a pay increase that gets you 40% of the way there, for example, shade four cells.

Housing Cost – For your Housing Cost Decrease, subtract your Current Cost from your Goal Cost and enter the amount you need to decrease this expense by. As you complete each of the three steps you decided were necessary to successfully achieve this reduction, shade in one cell.

PART TWO: TWELVE MONTH REBALANCE

Visual Progress Tracker

Progress		Progress	
	$_____ One-Year Goal		$_____ One-Year Goal
	Security Cushion Goal ↑ $_____		**Spending Reduction** Goal ↓ $_____
	$_____ Monthly Goal		$_____ Monthly Goal

Progress		Progress	
	$_____ One-Year Goal		$_____ One-Year Goal
	Investments Goal ↑ $_____		**Debt Reduction** Goal ↓ $_____
	$_____ Monthly Goal		$_____ Monthly Goal

Progress		Progress	
	$_____ Target Income	Step Three	$_____ Goal Cost
	Career Income Increase ↑ $_____	Step Two	**Housing Cost** Decrease ↓ $_____
	$_____ Current Income	Step One	$_____ Current Cost

Current Net Worth $_____   Target Net Worth $_____

Net Worth Goal Progress: ☐☐☐☐☐☐☐☐☐☐

Net Worth Increase Goal $_____

Income Distribution Plan

Use this form to create your monthly income distribution action plan. You may need to update this along the way should your income increase or decrease. Use this every time you get paid to simplify your distributions and ensure you are following your rebalance blueprint.

Income Distribution Plan (Twelve-Month Rebalance)

Weekly Income

Total Income	Week Number
$ _____	1
$ _____	2
$ _____	3
$ _____	4
Income Monthly Total $ _____	

Distribution Category and Payment Destinations

Cushion (savings)	Housing (checking)	Necessities (checking)	Personal (checking and cash)	Investments (direct deposit)	Fun Money (cash)	Hit List (pay vendor)
$ _____	$ _____	$ _____	$ _____	$ _____	$ _____	$ _____
$ _____	$ _____	$ _____	$ _____	$ _____	$ _____	$ _____
$ _____	$ _____	$ _____	$ _____	$ _____	$ _____	$ _____
$ _____	$ _____	$ _____	$ _____	$ _____	$ _____	$ _____
Cushion Monthly Total $ _____	Housing Monthly Total $ _____	Necessities Monthly Total $ _____	Personal Monthly Total $ _____	Investments Monthly Total $ _____	Fun Money Monthly Total $ _____	Debt Monthly Total $ _____

PART TWO: TWELVE MONTH REBALANCE

Maximizing Your Results

Now that you have created an action plan to transition in to a Wealth Builder Lifestyle, where do you go from here? As you live your new lifestyle you will constantly be tested and have to make numerous financial decisions, some small, some major, but they will all have an impact on your wealth building success. In Part Three we are going to look at ten essential wealth builder strategies and decision making tools that will support your wealth building efforts.

By using these ten wealth builder essentials, you will create an environment that will foster financial success. Incorporating the following characteristics into your lifestyle as well as using the appropriate tools when applicable will help maximize the results you get from living a Wealth Builder Lifestyle.

NOTES :

PART THREE:
WEALTH BUILDER ESSENTIALS

INVESTING 101

Investing is one of the most prevalent difference between those who are rich (or becoming rich) and those who are not. If you want to get on track for the former, start investing now regardless of how much or what the method involves. Just start investing.

That may sound like reckless financial advice, but if you are not already investing, you likely have little to no money set aside working to build wealth for you. Furthermore, if you look five years into your past you probably had the same amount saved or invested as you do right now. And if you make no change, five years from now you will *still* have the same. So no matter the circumstances, just start consistently investing even a small amount now.

Sure, if you put no effort in to making at least a semi-informed investment, you may lose 100% of it. That wouldn't be good, but as long as you make reasonable efforts to avoid that when making your decisions, that's not very likely. Worst-case scenario, you would only end up where you currently are today. The risk of not making forward progress is far higher when you choose not to invest at all. Don't let the fear of not being a good investor or of potentially taking a loss chain you to a life of servitude.

There are three investment categories that the Wealth Builder Lifestyle promotes, and I'll share some of the vehicles you may want to use for each of these categories. You should never put all your money in to any one investment, especially not a high-risk, high-growth one. That's a fool's idea of smart! Don't let your emotions get the best of you when you see the possibilities.

I am not a certified investment advisor, so keep in mind that these concepts are my opinions only and may not be right for you. That being said, these investment strategies have been used very successfully by some of the best know wealth builders. If you choose to invest in anything that you are not fully competent in, you should seek out the required training to get educated and be up to speed so that you can make informed decisions. You can take classes, hire an advisor, or do research on your own, but ultimately any investment decisions are your sole responsibility. I'll end with one last caveat: there are some good financial experts and some bad ones, so either way you go you really need to do your own homework to fully understand any deals you are going to make.

Security Investments

These can be things like cash, precious metals, your home, and low-risk growth mutual funds. Your goal is to average a 7% annual return with very minimal risk.

PART THREE: WEALTH BUILDER ESSENTIALS

Growth Investments

My preferences here include mutual funds in the following three categories: growth and income, aggressive growth, and international. These are not the only options, but keep in mind that your primary goal here is to get a return in excess of 10% without substantial risk.

Business Investments

Some options for this investment class are purchasing aggressive growth mutual funds, directly funding someone else's business, or investing in a business of your own. Your goal is to generate a return in excess of 15%, and to do this you are likely going to have to take on more risk. That is why these are called *business* investments. No business can guarantee profit, but that's why they have the potential to generate higher than normal returns.

I'm a skeptic of "expert" advice when it comes to investments, and you should be too. There is no shame in applying a healthy dose of skepticism when interacting with anyone doling out financial advice. When it comes to my money, I'm the only expert I trust. I go out of my way to get the best possible information from the best possible sources when evaluating whether something is truly worthy of my financial investment.

Throughout the recent financial crisis, I watched the majority of the talking heads and so-called experts on TV give out some of the worst advice of the 21st century. This advice surely lead to substantial financial losses for anyone that followed it.

I advise you to read books or take training courses by qualified experts as you get started. You don't have to be an expert yourself, but growing your expertise over time will help you be a more competent and successful investor. Eventually this will also help you keep any financial experts you hire in check.

Following are five things I think you should consider when trying to find a financial expert to represent your interest.

Credentials

If someone claims to be a financial expert, they had better be able to support their claim. Not only that, but there are varying degrees in this category: CPAs, RIAs, CFPs, CFAs, and all kinds of other acronyms. The term financial expert is used loosely, but includes many levels of expertise and specialty. As a comparison, just because someone has expert training in the medical field doesn't mean they are qualified to do open heart surgery.

Where's the Money?

Financial advisors do what they do for a reason: to make money. There's nothing wrong with them making money, but you need to know where and how they will be making it off of you

INVESTING 101

so you can evaluate their investment approach. If they are a fiduciary, they have to place their client's best interests ahead of their own and disclose how they are compensated. Although their obligation to make you aware of how they are compensated is good, I'm not necessarily saying a fiduciary is the way to go. After all, such a decision may actually limit your wealth building potential due to the reduced number of services they may be able to offer. The main thing is to evaluate their motivations for recommending certain investments. Don't be afraid to ask. It's your money and only you will truly look to protect it.

Cost

This may seem like the same thing we just covered, but it is different. The above question was primed at determining any background sources of income they might generate from directing your money into certain assets. The intention of this concern, however, is to understand how much you can anticipate their services costing you directly. This is important information for determining the total potential upside of working with them. Take for instance a $10,000 investment you make with a firm that historically returns around 13% per year. A $1,300 return on your investment isn't bad. On the other hand, if they are charging you a 5% management fee for handling the investment it will affect your overall return. In this case, the management cost would be $500. To calculate your real potential return, you need to subtract the fees ($500) from your return ($1,300). So the actual potential return of such an investment would be 8% or $800, which really isn't that great. Do your homework up front so you are not surprised later.

Track Record

Just like a pie-in-the-sky forecast, goals and expectations are all great but history is the most accurate predictor of the future. Find out what their historical returns have been, including proof for any investments they are pushing. Make sure the performance is not just for a one-year period (everyone gets a homerun every once in a while). I would look for at least a five-year track record that represents the results you want. Don't just ask once. If the advisor you choose suggests another investment instrument or approach, ask to see the five-year track record before agreeing to make the move. You can minimize your risk with proven results.

Fit and Strategy

It's not "one size fits all" when seeking the best fit for your goal and interest representation. This most often comes down to the strategy or approach of the financial expert or service. Some may represent large-dollar investors with several million invested (and therefore make them a priority), to whom you may seem like small potatoes. You're not likely to get the personal attention you want with a company like that. Or, you just may not relate to how they dress, act, and talk—they may be used to servicing a certain type of client that doesn't match who you are. If you're a new investor, you may want a smaller firm that can take the time to give you some personal attention and help you understand what it takes to get started. A company that will take the time to make sure your investment growth strategy is in line with your wealth-building plan is crucial. Working with an advisor or company that is a good fit and that provides the services that support your investment strategy can greatly enhance your results and comfort in working together.

Investing Resources

You do not necessarily need to hire an investment firm to make investments or manage your money for you. Those resources may help you feel more comfortable getting started but these days they are not required. With the internet you have access to a world of resources and information that allows anyone the ability to get informed and make their own investments.

The number one thing I hear that stops people from investing is that they just don't know how or where to go. These days, it truly couldn't be any easier. If you have never invested before or have limited investing experience, here are a few places you can go online for more information or to get started. All of these links will take you to online investment companies where you can easily setup an account within minutes. Most have no minimum investment to get started, but there may be one to open your IRAs. If that's the case, just contribute to your equities until you have enough invested to roll it over into an IRA.

These brokerages all provide their own investing resources (such as stock and fund performance histories) so you can easily do related research. Then once you are ready, select the fund or stock you want to buy, how many shares you want, then just click buy. In case you were unaware, stocks and mutual funds are sold in shares. Essentially, they're just tiny pieces of a business. The share cost varies by company, so if you want to buy $500 of a certain company then divide that amount by the individual share price to determine how many shares you should purchase.

TD Ameritrade - https://www.tdameritrade.com

Scottrade - https://www.scottrade.com

Etrade - https://www.etrade.com

Vanguard - https://investor.vanguard.com

The sources listed here are in no particular order. I have no affiliations or ties with any of them, they are just some of the most popular and easy to use options out there. You can also setup your online trading account to automatically transfer a set amount from your checking account each month. This can automate your investment contributions so you can effortlessly stay on track and meet your investing requirements. All of these online trading companies have very good support and instructions, so there is no need to be intimidated. You don't need to have any ninja investor credentials to be successful.

Investment Fund Flow

You want to make sure you fund the most beneficial investments first, so I'm going to present my recommendation. If you have the option of an employer-matched 401K, you will want to max that out first. Then fully max out your Roth and/or Traditional IRAs before rolling into your traditional mutual funds. Here is a little breakdown of why you want to fund in this particular order.

Employer-Matched 401K

This one should be pretty obvious: you make an immediate return on your investment of up to 100% of every dollar you invest, which is pretty hard to beat. Most employers will match up to a certain limit, so if possible you should contribute up to that amount.

Roth IRA

With a Roth IRA, you make post-tax contributions, so you invest out of your net income. The beauty of this is that when you start withdrawing in retirement your withdrawals will be tax-free. As you get closer to retirement, the importance of funding your Roth IRA will diminish because it will have less time to grow (negating the value of net investment dollars). If you do not have at least 15 years (preferably 20) to allow your Roth investment to grow before you touch them, the benefits for most users will be lost or at best a break even. As you get close to this being a consideration talk to your accountant or financial advisor to determine the best time for you to stop contributing to this investment tool.

Traditional IRA

Your contributions may be tax deductible; meaning the money you contribute would not be subject to income taxes. This means that what you would normally have to pay in income tax you could actually invest and earn interest on. However, when you finally make withdrawals at retirement, they will be taxed as income.

PART THREE: WEALTH BUILDER ESSENTIALS

Both IRAs

Many people will qualify for both IRA types, which have maximum annual contribution limits. They both have rules for early withdrawals, and in addition, a traditional IRA (currently) has mandatory distribution requirements beginning at the age of 70½. The reason you want to fund IRAs first is because you can still invest in similar instruments (like mutual funds), but the tax benefits make IRAs more attractive than just straight equity investments. So max them out if you can!

Traditional Mutual Funds

Invest in these last since they do not have matching or tax incentives. That doesn't make them bad, just not as great!

Keep the following flow chart below in mind when you are thinking about which investments to contribute to first.

Cash Flow Assets

Cash flow assets include (by definition) any asset that you invest in that increases your monthly or yearly income. Some assets (like your home) do not necessarily contribute to your cash flow but instead may increase your net worth. Focusing at least some of your investment money on assets that increase your monthly or at least yearly income in a way that is liquid builds financial strength. This will put you in a better position in the event of an income disruption or loss as you will have additional income sources.

INVESTING 101

A few options for cash flow assets are:

1. Income-producing rental properties
2. Stocks that pay dividends
3. Loans that receive interest-only payments until they are due in full

The last option is unique, but might be available when lending money to a business so they can cover their operating expenses until a particular receivable comes in.

There are some great books out there almost exclusively on the topic of cash flow investments. In particular, Robert Kyosaki has a few great resources in his Rich Dad series of books.

Always remember to stay diversified, don't get overleveraged, and consistently work at building your net worth. I don't support the approach of any "financial guru" that pushes people to get too close to the edge in an attempt to get rich. Those strategies can take all the progress from years of good wealth building efforts and quickly destroy everything you have been working for. That type of extreme wealth destruction comes from a get-rich-quick mentality that is overly greedy and money centric.

Money – A Silent Employee

The way I look at *every* dollar is that each has the potential to be a hassle-free, silent employee. If you don't want to own a business I can totally understand, but I still think we all need something consistently working for us to build wealth. Investments give us the opportunity to leverage something small today that will grow and mature into something much greater later on in life. Every time you spend a dollar, think of that action as permanently firing one of your potential employees. That employee would have been more than happy to work and build wealth for you for a lifetime without complaint.

If you haven't already gotten excited about investing or at least come to the conclusion that you need to and should be consistently investing over the long term, take a look at these little facts. You are likely over 18, but I want you to see the real power of investing. If you put away just $1 at age 18 into an investment that averages a 12% annual return, when you retire at 65 that one dollar will be worth $205 dollars. So say instead of moving out you live at home with your parents for one extra year and work a job—any job, even one for minimum wage. Then you contribute $430 a month over the next twelve months (a grand total of $5,160) to an investment with an anticipated 12% annual return. At the age of 19, your net worth would probably exceed 99% of your peers', and even if you never invested another cent, by the time you reach age 65 you could be a millionaire.

This is absolutely possible due to the power of compound interest (which we will cover more in the next section) but before I move on let's look at one more scenario. Let's say when your kid is born you invest $1,000 one time into an investment account returning 12%. If you contribute nothing else, by the time your child is ready to head out to college you will end up with an investment amount of about $7,690. Not bad—after all, your investment did increase by almost 8 times its original worth. Now, let's say you are a strict parent trying to instill a good work ethic in your child by making them find their own way to pay for college. Instead of pulling that money out, you just leave that money to sit in a trust until they retire at 65. That one-time $1,000 investment would end up being worth $1,582,000.

Why with all this opportunity in the world are so many people retiring broke? It's because they either don't take the time to get even a basic financial education or they procrastinate and don't take the necessary actions. It's never too late. If you haven't started, look at the potential in these opportunities and get started today. Furthermore, if you are a parent or will be a parent you need to teach your kids about wealth building while they are young. Do your kids a favor and don't send them out into the world foolishly unprepared when I just showed you two simple ways that you can help make sure your kids retire millionaires. The most expensive of those options would only cost you $1,000, and I know your kids are worth it to you so take some action. Although, I guess in one of those scenarios you would have to keep them around for an extra year... Ah, suck it up, it's worth it!

The Compound Effect

We've briefly touched on this subject, but now I want to go a little more in-depth on the topic. The compound effect, unfortunately, cuts both ways. So it's important that you have a clear understanding of how it works and how you do or don't want it affecting your life. This concept is the primary reason why savers are losers and investors are winners.

We've all heard about inflation. It usually averages a few percent each year, around 2% to 4% annually. Savers and investors both need to keep this in mind, but the former need to even more so since they don't have any protection against inflation. This is one of the reasons why a home is more of a security investment rather than a growth investment. Historically (outside of boom markets, which always bust), home values tend to barely outpace inflation—if at all—which is really the way it should be.

You really need to focus on and beat the most blatant and unrelenting adverse compound-like effect that plagues us all: inflation. It may seem like 2 to 4% is a pretty small and harmless number unless you recognize it for what it truly is (an exponentially increasing rate). If it didn't increase at an exponential rate, that 3% average annual rise over thirty years would equate to a cost increase of 90% (30 × 3%). So that loaf of bread that cost $1 thirty

INVESTING 101

years ago would only cost $1.90 now. Sadly, that's not how it works. A 3% inflation rate over thirty years actually amounts to an increase of 143% ($1.03^{30}-1.0$), so now your bread actually costs $2.43. Therefore, if you go the savings route, the dollar you save now will not even get you half of a loaf in thirty years. If, on the other hand, you invest in a 3% CD you will have protection against inflation and you will still be able to buy a full loaf come that time.

Figure out at what age you want to retire (for example, 65). Then subtract that from your estimated life expectancy (85 in our example case). I came up with 20 years, but of course your answer may differ. Then, multiply the lowest amount you could get by on right now by the number of years your last calculation came to (20 for me). We will assume that a reasonable annual living equals $24,000, or $2,000 a month. This example also assumes you are thirty years from retirement.

Example:

    Step 1:   85 - 65 = 20 years

    Step 2:   20 × $24,000 = $480,000

Your numbers:

    Step 1: _____ - _____ = _____

    Step 2: _____ × _____ = _____

That's the amount you would need to save for retirement if there was no inflation. Now, let's assume our inflation rate of 3% is accurate so I can give you an idea of how much you will *really* need to save.

Example:

Desired annual allowance: **$24,000**

Years until retirement: **30**

Total required (no inflation): **$480,000**

Total required on retirement day (based on a 3% inflation rate): **$1,165,000**

Yikes! Inflation is insane, is it not? This calculation is just accounting for the inflation that will occur between now and when our example retires (in our case, 30 years). Unfortunately, it doesn't stop there.

Not only do we have to account for those extra years, but due to inflation's compound-like nature the numbers get dramatically worse much quicker. You may find it hard to believe, but that's the actual amount someone in the example situation would have to save to be able to retire at their current standard of living. Unfortunately, the math on that

PART THREE: WEALTH BUILDER ESSENTIALS

one is relatively complex (thanks to the compound effect), so there is no simple equation for me to share with you that would allow you to perform your own specific calculation.

So, based on our example you would have to save $52,200 per year for 30 years to save for a retirement equal to your current standard of living. I'm going to make a wild assumption here and say that most people with a baseline of $24,000 do not have the ability to save $52,200 a year for retirement, which is exactly why savers are losers in the long run.

Now, just for kicks let's look at a simple counter-example using the compound effect in our favor by investing. You would only need to invest $510 a month ($6,120 a year) for 30 years into an investment account earning a 12% return to exceed that $1,566,000. That is the amount you would have when you reached the age of 65. Sounds pretty nice, right? Well hold on, it gets much better! You could pull an annual income of nearly $200,000 off of that investment without touching a single penny of your $1.6 million principal!

Your desired $24,000 retirement lifestyle would be costing you an inflation-adjusted $81,600, so you would have exceeded your goal by over double while only investing $183,600. Not only that, but when you die you will still be a millionaire. Even if you had miraculously saved the amount you needed instead of going the investment route, you would still die broke at 85. Moreover, if you did happen to live longer, you would have a serious financial problem.

The important part here is to just start investing, don't chance it or assume you can save your way to a great retirement. The first step is the hardest, but once you start investing you will quickly get more familiar with how these things work. Soon you will see just how simple it is to invest and grow your money and wonder why you ever feared you couldn't do it.

I encourage you to accept the notion that you can't possibly save enough money to retire. Even if you could save up the amount you needed, it would be foolish to let inflation constantly erode your wealth while your money is just sitting. If you take the few simple steps required to invest your money, not only will it grow to offset the negative effects of inflation, it will generate more free wealth you won't have to work for.

"Through your habits you can choose to live the lifestyle of the rich and famous or the poor and destitute. Only you can decide!"

- Daniel Hartjoy

PERSONAL FINANCE IS YOUR BUSINESS

Operate your personal financial life like a business. Your personal financial life must turn a profit so you can afford to sustain the occasional loss. Our lives are governed under the same principles as a business. You can't go through life just breaking even or you'll never move ahead, always teetering on the verge of failure. Businesses have to make a profit for survival, and people also need to be making a profit and putting those profits back to work for them to build a better future and a strong safety net. When someone files bankruptcy, it's typically because they treated their financial life like a poorly-run business with no profit, no reinvestment, and no security cushion.

Do yourself a big favor and don't live on the edge of financial ruin. Structure your financial life to consistently earn a profit and then re-invest to build a rock-solid financial future of security and prosperity.

Financial Peace of Mind

Don't forget your security cushion. It may not seem like a great wealth building tool as the compound-like effects of inflation work against it, but it's your insurance policy against rough patches you **will** eventually have.

When you know you are consistently building wealth and have a nice chunk of cash sitting in your bank account, you will feel financially strong and secure. Just think for a moment of how you would feel with twelve months' worth of your living expenses sitting in the reserve. How would you feel knowing that if you lost your job, got injured, or had some other unexpected expense come up that you could cover it without having to sell off your assets, run up your credit cards, or stress about how you are going to get by? *That* is truly having peace of mind.

NOTES :

_____

_____

_____

_____

FINANCIAL FENG SHUI: YOUR ENVIRONMENT

Some of the most powerful and easy to harness forces that can help get you moving in the Wealth Builder Lifestyle are in your surrounding environment. These natural forces are continually working for or against you without any conscious effort on your part. It's important to take some steps to make sure you are living primarily in environments that are pushing and pulling you in a positive direction. You also need to try to minimize any counterproductive environmental forces.

Personal Associations

One of the most powerful types of environmental forces are your personal relationships. Consider that you are best represented by the average of the five people you spend the most time around. Right now we are specifically talking about your wealth, so look at the wealth status of those people. Are their financial statuses reminiscent of the results you are after? Are their net worth, debt, and income values in line with what you hope to achieve? Are they living lifestyles that continually increase their level of wealth?

If you can't answer yes to these three questions, you need to come up with a plan to realign your key personal associations. This one change can help get you moving in the right direction.

In the following space, make a list of the five people that represent lifestyles you *don't* want to gravitate towards. You should reduce or even consider eliminating your time with these acquaintances (if they are not positively influencing your life in some way).

Five people I need to limit exposure to or cut associations with completely:

1. _____
2. _____
3. _____
4. _____
5. _____

PART THREE: WEALTH BUILDER ESSENTIALS

Now list the five people that you want to build relationships with or focus on spending more time with. If you can't come up with that many, expand your friend base.

Five people I need to include in my key group of associations:

1. _____
2. _____
3. _____
4. _____
5. _____

Don't underestimate the power of good associations. They will pull you effortlessly in their direction—whether good or bad—so make sure their direction is ultimately aligned with the one you desire.

Physical Associations

Next, you need to look at your physical environment. Most people choose things like where they live, work, dine, go for recreation, and so on based on things other than their financial goals. These environmental associations can have a dramatic impact on your fiscal prosperity. Could you imagine someone that wants to become a surfing champion living in Alaska? Maybe these people could achieve their dreams, but there would be some major obstacles working against them based solely on their physical location. Examine your life and consider if you may not be in the best physical location to meet your goals.

Your physical environment is not just about where you live. It also includes things like where you spend your time outside your home. For instance, dining in an atmosphere filled with people that are living the lifestyle you seek can help you take on the image of someone similar. This will also put you in an environment to make positive contacts and friends.

Some other great environmental resources for achieving this are seminars, classes, and clubs. If you want to become a real estate investor, taking some classes or attending a seminar can not only provide you with an abundance of knowledge on the subject but also surround you with similar-minded individuals.

If you live in a bad area with high crime or few economic opportunities but can't currently afford to move, making the extra effort to travel outside your neighborhood could pay off big. Performing your work and social interactions in an area that is more prosperous

FINANCIAL FENG SHUI: YOUR ENVIRONMENT

greatly increases your chances of breaking out and creating a better lifestyle for yourself. If someone who has the deck stacked against them just packed up and moved to an area filled with better people and opportunities, odds are they would get caught up in the current of the average standards of that area and have their life changed forever.

Most people that come from a disadvantaged area tend to believe that how they currently live would be the same no matter the location. That belief is probably accompanied by the thought that they could never survive in an area filled with high achievers. Those beliefs create a predetermined fate and are the chains that will bind them, keeping them stuck right where they are. If that's you, I challenge you to discard those beliefs and take action. If you cross the tracks into that new environment, I know you can succeed regardless of the obstacles.

It all starts with the boldness to believe you can and that life has more to offer you than what you currently have. Think through how your current physical environments may be limiting you and what changes (big or small) could put you in better ones that will help cultivate your success.

Make a list of five environmental changes you will make that will put you in areas that support your goals and provide opportunities for success (or at least allow you to socialize with people that have achieved the success you desire).

Five changes I will make to my physical environment that supports my new goals:

1. _____
2. _____
3. _____
4. _____
5. _____

Sometimes the most powerful thing we can do is keep ourselves out of the environments that support our old habits that have prevented us from succeeding. If your plan involves cutting your costs on discretionary expenses like coffee, don't schedule to meet your friends at your favorite coffee shop. There are other places with comfortable chairs to hang out. What are some strong contributors to your failure to change your bad habits that are working against you?

PART THREE: WEALTH BUILDER ESSENTIALS

Five physical environments I will not go to that are keeping me from achieving my goals:

1. _____
2. _____
3. _____
4. _____
5. _____

NOTES :

YOUR IMAGE

Do you have any bad financial habits? Here's an amazing example of how five little habits that most of us have will end up costing us a million dollars in wealth over our lifetime.

A Million Dollars of Bad Habits		
The Bad Habits	Wealth Waster Lifestyle	Wealth Builder Lifestyle
Coffee Budget	$20	$8
Cell Phone	$130	$65
Movie Service	$9	$0
Cable	$75	$0
Dining Out	$30	$0
Total Habit Costs	*$264*	*$73*
	Total Monthly Savings	*$191*

The example above is based on: cutting back one specialty coffee drink per week to just regular coffee; utilizing a pre-paid smart phone instead of the latest trendy device on a contract plan; cutting your internet-based movie service; dropping cable; and reducing your regimen of dining out by one time a month (not eliminating it, just cutting one time).

How will you ever get by without all that cool stuff? Very well, actually! Not only will you set yourself up to have a million dollars when you retire (which will be really awesome), but you will also be cutting unproductive time spent behind a television or computer screen. This will free up more time to do some things that can add real value to your life, like maybe taking a class that will improve your career options.

Now, let's have some fun doing a little math. Let's say we start this cut-back at age 30. We are saving $191 a month, so by the time we are 65 (420 months later) we will have saved **$80,220** (420 × $191). That's not a million dollars! Wait, there is one more bad habit I forgot to put on the list: **not investing**. We are not going to just save that $191, we are going to contribute it monthly to an income and growth mutual fund with a target return of 12%. By doing so we get some new math that looks like this: 420 × $191 = **$1,053,000**. And there you have it! A million dollars, generated just by changing a few bad habits.

PART THREE: WEALTH BUILDER ESSENTIALS
Wealth Building Superstar

Ok, so maybe using the term "superstar" is over-glamorizing a wealth builder's image, but the picture you maintain internally and externally will affect your ability to build wealth. How you see yourself and how others see you helps define the way people interact with you and the opportunities that will be presented to you.

If you are someone that is loose with money and always willing to pick up the tab, you will have many opportunities coming your way to do just that. If, on the other hand, when people go out to lunch with you they know they will have to let go of their own hard-earned money, they likely will not be so eager to go on as many lunch dates (consequently saving you a lot of money). If you are someone that people know is always looking for a good financial opportunity to grow your wealth, you will be amazed at how many prospects will appear seemingly out of nowhere.

If you see yourself as someone that spends too much who will never be able to build wealth, you are not likely to save money or look for investment opportunities simply because of your self-perception. On the other side of that coin, if you see yourself as a penny-pinching power investor you are not going to easily let go of money and you will be continually looking for investment opportunities. Write a brief description of your current wealth builder image. How do you currently view yourself when it comes to wealth building? How do you believe others see you?

How do you currently feel and think about money and wealth building?

_____

_____

_____

_____

How do others view you in regards to money and wealth building?

_____

_____

_____

_____

YOUR IMAGE

Do you think these internal and external images define someone who is destined to be financially successful? Do these descriptions match how you would envision someone you know who is financially successful? Do you believe your current descriptions empower you and support your attempt to build wealth?

Write out descriptions for a new empowering image that supports your desired wealth building goals. How do you need to see yourself? What traits do you need to emanate to those around you? Think about how the people you know who are already successful act and the attitude they display regarding wealth and money. Then think of how you would act and the attitude you would have if you were already a millionaire.

With your new image, how would you feel and think about money and wealth building?

_____

_____

_____

_____

With your new image, how would others view you in regards to money and wealth building?

_____

_____

_____

_____

Your Personal Slogan

Create an empowering, memorable slogan that represents your new wealth builder image. Take into consideration your biggest weaknesses and the things you need to do different. It can be as long or as short as you want, just keep it simple and easy to remember.

My personal wealth builder slogan:

_____

_____

YOUR FOCUS

It is always important to maintain your focus on the things that impact your dreams the most. By this point you should have a pretty clear idea of where you're doing well and where you need the most improvement. Based on your personal situation, determine the three personal keys that are the most important for you to maintain focus on to become a successful wealth builder. Once again, keep them simple and memorable. Essentially, these will be your new operating guidelines.

Things to do More of

These are the items you want to do more of: saving, investing, improving your income, building assets, paying down debt, etc. Write out your new "to-do" list for building wealth.

My personal points to do more of:

1. _____
2. _____
3. _____

Things to Minimize

These are the things you may need to do sometimes, that don't really serve your wealth building lifestyle. Write out your new "to-limit" list for things to keep to a minimum (excessive discretionary spending, unnecessary driving, and so on).

My personal points to minimize:

1. _____
2. _____
3. _____

PART THREE: WEALTH BUILDER ESSENTIALS

Things to Eliminate

These are things that destroy or greatly hurt your wealth building potential that should be totally eliminated. Write out your new *never*-to-do list for things to avoid at all costs (use credit cards, take on more debt, and so on).

My personal points to eliminate:

1. _____
2. _____
3. _____

NOTES:

_____
_____
_____
_____
_____
_____
_____
_____
_____
_____
_____
_____
_____
_____

LIVE IN THE MOMENT: SPEND IN THE PAST OR FUTURE

Most people focus on earning, saving, and investing for wealth building. Although all of those are great actions that almost everyone has the ability to do, many end up outspending their progress. It takes discipline to keep tight reigns on the money and not erode your progress. Unfortunately, training self-restraint is often easier said than done.

So the "live in the moment, spend in the past or future" strategy is meant to cause interference in your spending. Using this strategy can greatly reduce or eliminate your impulse purchases and emotional spending. It also increases the chances you will get the best deals and stretch the dollars you do decide to spend.

So what does it mean to spend in the past or future? Essentially, you will do away with spending in the moment. If you want to go on a vacation, you will not monetize your plans when you decide you want to go. Instead, you will give yourself a cooling off period, a time more commonly spent going through buyer's remorse from poor financial decisions. We don't necessarily need to use discipline to walk away. Instead we can use the distraction of planning to buy us some time to come to our senses and understand the true impact of the decision before pulling the trigger. This is not about making the decision of whether to spend or not to spend, only about creating a delay that gives you the time to make sure your decision supports your lifestyle and goals.

A good decision involves making sure the purchase is in line with your overall plan. You need to make sure you can actually afford it and that you've taken the time to research the best possible deal available. This way, you are sure to get the best value for the money you spend. Maybe you want to take a vacation and it does ultimately turn out to be in line with your plan. Delaying and waiting to spend in the future gives you time to make sure it's well planned, intelligently purchased, and within the financial budget you have allocated.

The result is that you end up not spending "in the moment." You delay awhile and end up spending in the future. When you are on your vacation, you will be enjoying money that you actually spent in the past. There's no instant gratification here. It may just sound like word mumbo jumbo, but it can have a serious effect on your ability to build wealth.

Research has shown that there are many great benefits that come from delayed gratification. Even practicing this with your children can be very beneficial to their overall success in life. People that have low impulse control and frequently succumb to needs for instant gratification are far more likely to have high levels of debt, low self-discipline, and an attitude that they don't need to put in effort to get what they want. All of those characteristics are key ingredients for financial and personal underachievement. The good thing is that they can all be changed with a little effort.

Spending for Stimulation

Spending just to obtain stimulation has become an epidemic in our society. Not only do we not want to wait for gratification, but we also have a desire for constant stimulation that we look to gain from expending money. We seek it for enjoyment but the happiness it grants rarely lasts, which leads to a life of continual spending in an attempt to feed an insatiable desire.

Think about all the things you bought and what your motivation for purchasing them was. Was your spending to obtain some short-term stimulation like watching a movie? If so, consider cutting some of that spending by finding new ways to entertain yourself.

This will not only help you save money but can also have substantial rewards like building your creativity skills, of which there has been a dramatic reduction of here in the US. It was creativity and invention that made the US such a remarkable success, and it's the loss of those talents and abilities that will erode the future value of this great nation. Creativity is like a muscle: it needs exercise to get stronger.

In today's modern society we have an abundance of people relying on other people's creativity to provide us with amusement instead of being creative and generating it for ourselves. Consider your stimulation sources throughout a twelve-hour day. Where do they come from? Did you produce them, or were they products created by others such as movies, video games, television shows, YouTube videos, newspapers, amusement parks, alcohol, drugs, and so on?

This may seem a little bit off the topic of building wealth, but being successful in business or a career often hinges on your ability to be creative, ingenuitive, or think outside the box in some other way. This is also an important element in overcoming poor, stimulation-seeking spending habits. Use of your imagination can often times lead to entertainment without a high price tag, this can help you live a more full life at a greatly reduced cost.

NOTES :

_____

_____

INTELLECTUALIZING YOUR MONEY HABITS

Intellectualize your money habits by taking the emotion out of spending, borrowing, earning, and investing. What does that mean, exactly? Most people who are financially challenged are making financial decisions based on the emotion of the moment in an attempt to try and achieve a certain feeling they desire. By intellectualizing these tasks we can take the emotion out of them. Our monetary actions must fall in line with our well thought out wealth building plan, not our short-term desires for a particular feeling.

I'm not saying we should become mathematical robots... After all, emotions are what truly living is all about. I just want you to implement a strategy that will help keep your finances off the emotional roller coaster ride. Although some people make big, obvious mistakes that set them back financially, most people have a far more subtle method of destroying their fiscal future.

If it's small things that cause us big trouble, shouldn't that make it easier to fix? That may sound all and well but isn't necessarily the case. You will work hard to avoid big losses, but if you do happen upon one you will surely feel the pain and remember it for a long time. This natural form of punishment can make it far easier to maintain your focus and avoid a repeat. The wealth building game can be easily won or lost due to small decisions, especially for people with limited incomes. So to win the money game, we need to focus on the small underestimated aspects. When you look at the value of a dollar, for example, you can see how little things can add up to huge financial differences.

While some people will hesitate to spend $100, they can more easily justify multiple small purchases. These simple justifications can often add up to well over the $100 they were trying to avoid spending in the first place. Have you ever looked at your bank statement and thought, "Where'd the money go?" You look over the entire list and not one purchase was over $100, yet somehow $500 or even $1,000 is gone. If you look closer, you're bound to see the many infamous $17 coffee shop charges that you made to comfort yourself about not making that big purchase. Now your good feelings are gone and the negative despair has set in because you are once again broke. In the end, you got a few momentary pleasures while you were financially stepping backwards.

That was feel-good emotional spending—not an intellectualized financial decision. An intellectualized financial strategy will include provisions for your emotional satisfaction but in a way that is in balance with your overall financial goals. That's all we want: just

PART THREE: WEALTH BUILDER ESSENTIALS

balance. You *can* achieve a great life and emotional balance by making habits that don't set you back financially.

We all have moments of emotional weakness. They come in many forms and work to destroy us financially, and yet they are typically small and pervasive. We are often inclined to make foolish money moves out of guilt, our desire to feel good, or in an attempt to help others. Sometimes an effort to make financial progress even makes us vulnerable to deals that are actually too good to be true.

Take, for example, a member of your family that often comes to you to borrow money and that you know is always broke. You don't need to loan them money, and you probably shouldn't. Loaning money to someone you know is not likely to pay you back can make you just as financially "wise" as they are. The end result is you both will likely end up broke.

I know this can be hard with family, but we need to look at our money decisions intellectually. If you come from a poor family or have poor friends, the last thing you want to do is take financial advice from them, loan them money, or live your life in a similar fashion. So many people end up unintentionally adopting the bad behavior of those with whom they surround themselves with, eventually picking up poor financial habits by some crazy form of osmosis.

If osmosis is going to dominate the game, then I want to hang around people that know how to handle money and pick up *their* habits, not the other way around. When you think, "Should I loan money to this person that is broke and obviously has poor financial habits?" Thoroughly think that decision through. You will find that 99% of the time the answer is no.

If you are not (and have not previously been) wealthy, the odds are already stacked against you. It will become an impossible battle if you start taking on and covering the costs of those around you. Without a doubt, looseness of that kind will lead to your financial doom.

If you don't have money, you likely understand better than most the pain of not having it. Consequently, you may be very inclined to attempt to help others out when they are struggling. This is a noble cause, and giving is very rewarding (I greatly encourage it), but splitting your last dollar is not going to help anyone out. It will just create two losers. The best way to help someone who is financially struggling is not to give them money, but rather to be a good role model. Share what you learn here and show them the way to financial prosperity. Show them how they can intellectualize their financial habits and not give in to moments of emotional weakness.

INTELLECTUALIZING YOUR MONEY HABITS

People will often look at the rich and think they are greedy because they partake in so much while others hurt financially. However, anyone that understands money knows that giving to people with bad money habits will only lead to *everyone* being broke. On average, rich people give far more to good causes than people who aren't (and I'm not talking about the total dollar amount, but rather as a percentage of their wealth). They typically do it in a way that provides opportunities for people to improve their own lives, not to just improve it *for* them. Giving in a way that helps lead someone to improving their own situation provides dignity to the receiver and creates an environment with more opportunities for everyone.

There's an old Chinese proverb that says: **"Give a man a fish and he will eat for a day; teach a man to fish and he will eat for a lifetime."**

What I hope you will take from this is that everyone needs to know how to fish, so to speak. One of the best ways to learn is by teaching, so convey this information to those around you who might need to learn some of your proverbial fishing skills. Only a fool would give a fish to someone who is unwilling to learn to fish for themselves.

Living a poor life because you gave everything you have away, regardless of the good intention, does not make you a better person—only a poor one. By being financially successful and leading by example you will be able to afford to do far more good that will last.

NOTES :

_____

_____

_____

_____

_____

_____

_____

_____

_____

_____

ASSET ALLOCATIONS SIMPLIFIED

Improper asset allocation can unnecessarily leave the door open for wealth destruction. It can possibly even bring devastation to someone who appears very financially successful. The Wealth Builder program guidelines give you broad directions as to how you want to allocate your assets, but you need to think your allocations through even further.

Although there are some exceptions to the rule, a very diverse asset allocation approach will be best for most people. The average person should not dump a substantial amount of wealth into any one asset class, regardless of how great the opportunity. If anyone tells you different, they are of the get-rich-quick mentality and I would seek your financial advice from another source.

The following are some general principles for allocating your assets.

Security Cushion

Your security cushion should be divided into different assets to protect its value. I advise you to divide your security cushion into three eventually equal categories, funding the first category fully, then the second, and lastly the third.

1. **Cash** - Cash should be stored in an interest-bearing savings account.
2. **Investments** – Liquid money market or low-risk mutual funds should be utilized.
3. **Precious Metals** – Personally, I like owning physical gold and silver as opposed to electronically traded funds (ETFs). The primary drawback of owning precious metals physically is the buying and selling transaction costs. That being said, you are looking to hold on to this long term for a rainy day so it shouldn't be an issue. I said to invest in the other two categories first because this will be the last asset accessed should you need it.

Security Investments

Security investments should be all low-risk, including your home. Although some may not think of a home as a good investment anymore, you do need a place to live and if you have a mortgage then any additional investment you make into your home earns a return simply by saving you interest.

My personal favorite security investments are low-risk growth mutual funds (with a good track record of at least five years), Certificates of Deposit (CDs), and government-issued securities (savings bonds, treasury bonds, notes, and bills). The last two can be good options, but there are a couple of things to keep in mind: CDs don't usually outperform inflation adequately, and although government securities can appear safe, they can also be volatile. Also, government securities don't typically keep pace with the returns offered by mutual fund equities, but remember—this section is just about diversity to protect against individual assets taking hits.

Keep these three things in mind: diversity, liquidity, and inflation. You don't want to dump all your money into your home because that would be neither liquid nor diverse. Spread your investments around. If you only have a limited amount to invest, begin by investing in only one or two classes for four to six months and then alternate. Make sure your investments will outpace the rate of inflation, though, preferably by 3% or greater. I use 4% as my base rate of inflation (which may be high or low on some years but on average is probably a safe estimate).

Growth Investments

I think a diversified basket full of mutual funds from multiple categories is the best vehicle for this type of investment. Specifically, these three different kinds:

- Growth and income - ⅓
- Aggressive growth - ⅓
- International fund - ⅓

There are other investment allocation strategies out there, but I like this one because it is simple and fairly safe. As you approach retirement, consider cutting your aggressive growth holdings. When you are ten years from retirement, reduce your risky contributions by 20% each year. For your last five working years, reallocate 20% per year of the remaining aggressive growth balance in to safer funds.

ASSET ALLOCATIONS SIMPLIFIED
Business Investments

The primary goal here is either to get higher returns than mutual funds can provide or obtain better asset diversification. One vehicle for this entails investing directly into businesses (in the event that a good, relatively secure opportunity comes up). Another includes investing in real estate for the long hold or buying fixer-uppers to resell. Depending on your financial status, you may be able to buy established businesses that can be managed by others such as a bar, resort, recreational vehicle park, or other turnkey business.

Remember, it takes business savvy to own a business regardless of whether it will be managed by others or not. Business investments are not for everyone. You should not do something that you are uncomfortable with or that will put you at unnecessary risk. If the business class of investments is not right for you, just put your allocations into your more aggressive growth mutual funds.

NOTES :

MONEY-WISE AUTO-BUYING GUIDE

Cars have always been a terrible investment due to their depreciating nature, but there are things you can do to help minimize their wealth destruction. There are many different ways to evaluate car purchases, but here is the Wealth Builder Lifestyle's method.

Initial Depreciation

We all want and love new cars. They come with the pride of being the first owner of a vehicle, that great new car smell (which is created by the chemical off-gassing of the car's components, by the way), and the excitement of driving it home for the first time. This is an emotional motivation that has a high cost. Until you are so well off that you have money to burn, take this into consideration: you can expect the value of your new vehicle to drop by approximately 10% the minute you drive it off the lot and another 10% by the time you get a few miles on it. Plus there's the tax and licensing, which will run you about another 10%. So to experience the thrill of buying a $30,000 car new, could cost you $6,600 in the first few months of ownership. You had better really love that new car smell, because you paid a small fortune for it.

Fastest Depreciation

The first 36,000 miles (usually two to three years of age) has the second highest depreciation cost. You can expect this to create a loss of value of another 15-20% of the total value of your purchase. When thinking about depreciation, take into consideration that the second 36,000 miles will depreciate your value by only about half as much as the first (and similarly the third only half as much as the second). Therefore, the actual cash lost to depreciation for time and mileage is less and less as the vehicle gets older. You will always have depreciation costs no matter what automobile it is, but over time they may become negligible.

Many people buy new because they don't want to have to worry about breakdowns or repairs. This is a legitimate concern, but with the quality of cars built today the likelihood of a breakdown or major repair between 36,000 and 100,000 miles is actually very low. The Wealth Builder Lifestyle recommendation for people that want to drive new cars is to buy them when they are *virtually* new, so a few years old when the vehicle has around 36,000 miles on it. By this point, someone else has already taken the financial hit of the two largest depreciation periods.

PART THREE: WEALTH BUILDER ESSENTIALS
Cost of Ownership

Another aspect of car purchasing to be aware of is the cost of ownership, the biggest of which is usually fuel. We all want a vehicle that gets good gas mileage, but how important of a consideration is this for you? If fuel costs $3.25 a gallon and you drive 12,000 miles per year (which is an average value), a vehicle that gets 20 miles per gallon (MPG) will cost you $54 per month more to own than one that gets 30 MPG. Most people don't sweat the small dollars, so if you don't typically pay much heed to the MPG of a car you're not alone. Consider this: if you got the 30 MPG car and put the money you saved to work wealth builder style starting at the age of 18, then by the time you are 65, that little $54 monthly difference (a $30,500 total investment over the example period) could be worth $698,000 (based on a modest and achievable 10% return on investment).

Larger vehicles that get less miles per gallon will also usually cost more to maintain due to a larger oil capacity, bigger tires, and so on. I'm not saying bigger or smaller is better. They both have their pros and cons and for some situations there is no substitute for a superior vehicle.

One of the major goals I had for this program was to get people to start evaluating purchases with the lifetime cost in mind. My hope is that maybe then we will all have more appreciation for the true value of our money and financial decisions. Although $54 a month today doesn't seem like a big deal, it could get you over half way to retiring a millionaire. Use the following forms to help evaluate different car purchases. This can be an enlightening experience and if nothing else will help make you a more informed buyer.

We are going to evaluate your purchase in four areas:

- **Total purchase cost** – the total amount of cash you will actually spend to buy the car

- **Five-year depreciation** – the amount of the total purchase cost that the vehicle will lose in value over the next five years

- **Total monthly cost** – the estimated monthly cost for each option, including fuel, maintenance/repairs, and payments (adjusted by individual vehicle type)

- **Wealth impact** – how this will affect your long-term wealth picture (can vary greatly by vehicle)

MONEY-WISE AUTO-BUYING GUIDE

Use this form to determine the total overall purchase cost of a vehicle. If you are paying cash for the vehicle, just enter the total vehicle cost (including tax and license fees) in the Total Purchase Cost box. For an accurate comparison, any financed vehicles should be amortized over five years (although when you make your actual purchase I would obviously advise you to get as short of a loan as possible.)

Auto Purchase Analyzer			
Cost	Option One	Option Two	Option Three
Monthly Payment	$_____	$_____	$_____
Loan Length (in months)	× _____	× _____	× _____
Total of Payments (payment × months)	= $_____	= $_____	= $_____
Down Payment (plus any other cash expenses)	+ $_____	+ $_____	+ $_____
Total Purchase Cost (down payment + total of payments)	= $_____	= $_____	= $_____

NOTES :

_____
_____
_____
_____
_____
_____
_____
_____

PART THREE: WEALTH BUILDER ESSENTIALS

Use the Total Purchase Cost from the previous form in the following one. The depreciation (as it's known to most people) is evaluated by subtracting the End Value from the Purchase Price. A more realistic approach is to base it on the total amount of value left after all your purchase costs (which includes your financing cost). The difference between that and the End Value is the true loss you sustained on this vehicle over five years. Of course, no dealer or bank wants to point this out to you. Very few ever even consider it (much less calculate it), which is why so many have no idea how much wealth they are potentially wasting on vehicles.

Auto Comparison Overview				
Five-Year Depreciation Cost				
Rate Modifier Descriptions	ACMT average car or mini truck	LS luxury or sports car	S4X SUV or 4x4 truck	FS full size pickup or van
Brand New	ACMT = 0.45	LS = 0.35	S4X = 0.45	FS = 0.4
Used	ACMT = 0.5	LS = 0.3	S4X = 0.35	FS = 0.5
Option One _____	Purchase Price $_____	×	Total Purchase Cost = $_____ Rate Modifier _____ =	End Value $_____
Total Wealth Lost (Total Purchase Cost − End Value) = $_____				
Option Two _____	Purchase Price $_____	×	Total Purchase Cost = $_____ Rate Modifier _____ =	End Value $_____
Total Wealth Lost (Total Purchase Cost − End Value) = $_____				
Option Three _____	Purchase Price $_____	×	Total Purchase Cost = $_____ Rate Modifier _____ =	End Value $_____
Total Wealth Lost (Total Purchase Cost − End Value) = $_____				

The following form will help you get a better idea of the true monthly cost of purchasing and owning the different types of vehicles you are considering. There are a couple of key factors to consider regarding costs outside of the purchase price. Typically the larger and fancier the car the more it costs to operate and maintain.

MONEY-WISE AUTO-BUYING GUIDE

Detailed Auto Comparison

Annual Miles	Monthly Miles (annual ÷ 12)	Total Miles (annual × 5)	
_____	_____	_____	
Maintenance by Vehicle Type	ACMT = Compact or mid-sized car, compact truck LST = Luxury or sports car, SUV, 4×4, full size truck		
Less than 60,000 miles		ACMT = $0.04	LST = $0.07
60,000 to 120,000 miles		ACMT = $0.06	LST = $0.10
More than 120,000 miles		ACMT = $0.10	LST = $0.15

Option One

Fuel Cost per Gallon $_____	÷ MPG _____	= Cost per Mile	$_____
		Maintenance by Vehicle Type (from chart above)	$_____
		Fuel Cost per Mile + Maintenance by Vehicle Type	$_____
		Monthly Miles (from above)	_____
		(Fuel + Maintenance) × Monthly Miles	$_____
		Monthly Payment	$_____
		Total Monthly Cost (fuel and maintenance + payment)	$_____

Option Two

Fuel Cost per Gallon $_____	÷ MPG _____	= Cost per Mile	$_____
		Maintenance by Vehicle Type (from chart above)	$_____
		Fuel Cost per Mile + Maintenance by Vehicle Type	$_____
		Monthly Miles (from above)	_____
		(Fuel + Maintenance) × Monthly Miles	$_____
		Monthly Payment	$_____
		Total Monthly Cost (fuel and maintenance + payment)	$_____

Option Three

Fuel Cost per Gallon $_____	÷ MPG _____	= Cost per Mile	$_____
		Maintenance by Vehicle Type (from chart above)	$_____
		Fuel Cost per Mile + Maintenance by Vehicle Type	$_____
		Monthly Miles (from above)	_____
		(Fuel + Maintenance) × Monthly Miles	$_____
		Monthly Payment	$_____
		Total Monthly Cost (Fuel and Maintenance + Payment)	$_____

PART THREE: WEALTH BUILDER ESSENTIALS

Last but not least, we want to combine each of the previous variables to determine the overall wealth impact for each potential vehicle. The loss of potential wealth building opportunities is by far the most overlooked and damaging factor in making an auto purchase. The following will calculate the approx. difference based on investing any potential money saved over the five years and then letting it sit in a 10% return investment for 30 years.

Auto Wealth Impact Comparison

Option One

Highest Down Payment	Down Payment (option one)				Invested Value
$_____ −	$_____ =	$_____	× $28 =	$_____

Highest Monthly Cost	Monthly Cost (option one)				Invested Value
$_____ −	$_____ =	$_____	× $1,548 =	$_____

Total End Value (from depreciation form) $_____

Option One Total (combine all item totals) $_____

Option Two

Highest Down Payment	Down Payment (option two)				Invested Value
$_____ −	$_____ =	$_____	× $28 =	$_____

Highest Monthly Cost	Monthly Cost (option two)				Invested Value
$_____ −	$_____ =	$_____	× $1,548 =	$_____

Total End Value (from depreciation form) $_____

Option Two Total (combine all item totals) $_____

Option Three

Highest Down Payment	Down Payment (option three)				Invested Value
$_____ −	$_____ =	$_____	× $28 =	$_____

Highest Monthly Cost	Monthly Cost (option three)				Invested Value
$_____ −	$_____ =	$_____	× $1,548 =	$_____

Total End Value (from depreciation form) $_____

Option Three Total (combine all item totals) $_____

MONEY-WISE AUTO-BUYING GUIDE

Enter the requested information in the fields below to determine your final comparison results.

	Final Auto Comparison		
	Total (from previous)	Total Purchase Cost (page 187)	Total Wealth Impact
Option One	$_____	- $_____	= $_____
Option Two	$_____	- $_____	= $_____
Option Three	$_____	- $_____	= $_____

The higher the wealth impact number the better rated your vehicle is as a wealth builder. Some vehicles may actually come out a negative number (especially if you are only checking one car, since there is no difference that can be invested). I hope this has successfully illustrated the value of buying less than you can afford and investing the difference.

NOTES :

_____
_____
_____
_____
_____
_____
_____
_____
_____
_____

LUXURY PURCHASE ANALYSIS TOOL

We've talked about the adverse affects spending can have on wealth building primarily in regards to small purchases. Now we are going to talk about the real fun—big purchases like boats, RVs, and those other luxury items we buy when we start to get ahead financially.

It's a little ironic to me that when we finally start getting ahead, that's when we are most likely to make a huge purchasing mistake. Unfortunately, that one stroke of a pen can destroy large amounts of our net worth instantly.

There are six key points of consideration for wealth builders when it comes to making any large purchase.

Can you really afford it?

You need to ensure that when you purchase this you will still be able to make all of your saving and investment contributions in full as planned. If not, you can't afford it and a true wealth builder wouldn't buy it.

What will it cost to own?

Things like boats and RVs may require additional costs. You may need to insure it, pay taxes on it, store it, maintain it, and so on. All of those items are wealth eaters, so you need to be sure you can also afford to throw that money away.

What is the initial depreciation?

This is the total loss you will take the moment you sign the paperwork. If you are buying a new RV, for instance, the day you drive it off the lot it will likely lose about 20% in value, which comes directly off your net worth. So if you have $200,000 in net worth and go buy a $150,000 RV, the day you drive it off the lot it will depreciate $30,000 (plus whatever your initial tax, license, and other fees are) which will cause your net worth to instantly drop to less than $170,000. If you add that RV to your balance sheet at the purchase price, shame on you. You're only fooling yourself.

What is the future depreciation?

Most material possessions (outside of houses) are depreciating assets. Some are even quickly depreciating assets. A wealth builder will evaluate how long they plan to hold on to that RV, for example, and what they will be able to recover when they sell it. In the case of that

PART THREE: WEALTH BUILDER ESSENTIALS

$150,000 RV, I would estimate that after 15 years its market value (what you could actually sell it for) would be about $22,500, or 15% of what you paid for it. So your future depreciation would be another $97,500. Keep in mind, this doesn't include the interest you paid on the loan (if you financed it), storage, insurance, maintenance, or repair costs over those 15 years.

What is the total purchase cost?

Using the price of the item is not typically representative of the real cost because it doesn't include your finance charges.

What will this cost you in lost investment wealth?

This is probably one of the least looked at and most important considerations for a wealth builder. Being a wealth builder means you are continually growing your wealth. This means you not only have to offset any cost you spend, but you also have to look at the impact it has on your ability to generate wealth.

Use the following form to perform the desired calculations and to determine if you can afford the purchase. If you are buying a used item from a private party, you shouldn't have any initial depreciation. If you buy used from a dealer, use 10% for the initial depreciation factor (which assumes you negotiate and buy well) and 20% if you are buying new. Do a rough guestimate on the repair costs on the item during your time of ownership, divide that by the months owned, and include it in the Other category under Monthly Ownership Expenses.

NOTES :

_____

_____

_____

_____

_____

_____

_____

LUXURY PURCHASE ANALYSIS TOOL

Luxury Purchase Depreciation Evaluator

Purchase Price (excluding taxes and fees)	One-Time Fees (taxes, setup, deliver, etc.)	Total Purchase Cost (total initial purchase cost)
$ _____ +	$ _____ =	$ _____

Down Payment $ _____	Monthly Ownership Expenses Insurance $ _____ Tax and Reg. $ _____ Storage $ _____ Other $ _____	Combine the Monthly Ownership Expenses together and enter the monthly total at the bottom. Then, combine the Monthly Payment with the figure you just calculated to find the actual Total Monthly Cost.
Monthly Payment	Total Monthly Ownership Expenses	Total Monthly Cost
$ _____ +	$ _____ =	$ _____

Depreciation

Purchase Price (excluding tax and fees)	Depreciation Factor (estimated initial depreciation percentage)	Initial Depreciation
$ _____	× 0.00 (0%, for private party) 0.10 (10%, for dealer used) 0.20 (20%, for new) =	$ _____
Purchase Price - Initial Depreciation =	Blue Book Value at Resale (likely resale value)	+ Total Depreciation During Use
$ _____ -	$ _____ =	$ _____
		=

Total Lifetime Depreciation $ _____

To calculate the total impact the purchase will have on your wealth over the time span of ownership, complete the next form. It will require the use of amortization and compound interest calculators, which can easily be found online, or at the following links:

- http://www.interestcalc.org
- http://www.amortization-calc.com

PART THREE: WEALTH BUILDER ESSENTIALS

Don't short yourself by skipping this exercise as it's great knowledge for understanding how to evaluate a purchase of any kind. Once you understand this concept you can apply it to almost anything you buy to make better decisions. The person selling you something isn't going to help you look at the purchase this way, so learn how to do it yourself.

Luxury Purchase Wealth Impact Evaluator			
Amortization Calculation		**Compound Interest Calculation**	
Total Financed (loan amount)	$_____	Down Payment (initial investment)	$_____
Loan Length (in years)	_____	Interest Rate	10%
Interest Rate	_____%	Regular Investment (enter monthly ownership expenses)	$_____
Total Principle and Interest Payment	$_____	Loan Length (in years)	_____
Total Loan Cost	$_____	Total Investment Value	$_____
Combined Total (negative wealth impact)			$_____

The wealth impact is a little skewed because this amount is how much you would have by not making the purchase. If you actually did complete the transaction, you would still have a residual value equal to what that item could be sold for. You can run one more calculation for a more precise wealth impact evaluation by simply deducting the asset resale value from the total negative wealth impact. Just keep in mind that you also have the cost of use, this includes things like fuel or other related expenses that would be incurred while using the item. This is money that you would not be spending if you didn't make the purchase, so ultimately those would go against the asset resale value too.

Were you surprised at what the real cost of your purchase was? We are trained to always focus on the sticker price. Few (if any) people you asked could actually tell you what the real cost of making a purchase is. Now you will have the edge and can not only answer that question but also help educate friends and family so they too can make better purchasing decisions.

"BEAT THE BANK" HOMEOWNERSHIP

"Homeownership" and "bank" don't belong in the same sentence. The whole premise of owning your home is that you own it (and are therefore free of the bank). Where people usually go wrong in buying their home is in how they finance and pay off their loans. Here are some sample results for a $150,000 home that can be achieved with the method I'm going to share with you.

Typical Method

Time to Pay Off: **30 Years**

Sample Mortgage Amount: **$150,000**

Monthly Payment Based on 30 years at 5% APR: **$805.23**

Total Loan Interest Paid: **$139,884**

Total Cost to Pay off Loan: **$289,884**

Wealth Builder Method

Time to Pay Off: **15 Years**

Sample Mortgage Amount: **$150,000**

Accelerated Beginning Payment at 5% APR: **$986.21**

Accelerated Ending Payment at 5% APR: **$1,607.12**

Total Loan Interest Paid: **$70,098**

Total Cost to Pay off Loan: **$220,098**

Net Difference

1. Paid off 15 years sooner
2. $70,000 Less Interest Paid

Here is the Wealth Builder strategy for financing and paying off your home that will help you avoid the home buyer pitfalls that the banks prosper on. Work through the process of finding out exactly what the numbers would be on your home or on a home you may be considering buying.

PART THREE: WEALTH BUILDER ESSENTIALS

Here is a simple strategy that any homebuyer should be able to use and afford. This will allow you to greatly reduce the interest paid over the life of the loan and pay your home off in half the time. If you can't afford to use this strategy, you are probably not in a position to afford a house.

First, finance your home with a 30-year **fixed rate mortgage with no prepayment penalties**. The last part is very important. Some banks get you in to a loan and want to keep you there, reaping large profits as long as they can.

Our goal is to cut your loan repayment time in half without putting you on the edge financially (which is why I don't advise locking yourself in to a shorter term loan initially).

Next, collect the following information about your loan:

Current Loan Balance: $_____

Length left on loan: Years_____ Months_____

Your Loan Interest Rate: _____%

Current Payment: $_____

Then, you need to get an amortization schedule based on your loan terms; you can use an online calculator to create it (such as the one at http://www.amortization-calc.com). Enter values to the closest tenth of a year (for example if you have 26 and ½ years left enter it as 26.5). Then select "Amortization: show by month" and press Calculate. Printing this schedule out or saving it as a PDF would be helpful for future reference.

So here's how this method works: you are going to pay your regular monthly payment plus the principal portion of the following month's payment. For month one you will end up paying the full amount for the first month plus the principal of the 2nd, on month two you will pay your regular payment amount (which is what shows up for the 3rd month on your amortization schedule) plus the principal amount of the 4th month. An easy way to do this is to print out the amortization schedule and (starting with month two) highlight every other month. Each time you make a payment, work down the list of highlighted months and add that principal amount to your normal payment.

Note: You should check with your lender to see what specifically you need to do if anything to make a principle reduction payment. They may automatically apply the overpayment towards your principal balance, or they may (for example) want you to write a separate check with "pay towards principal" in the memo line.

"BEAT THE BANK" HOMEOWNERSHIP

Fill in your info to come up with the next twelve months of payments. Use the principal amount from your amortization schedule for the month advised in this form.

Accelerated Mortgage Payment Schedule			
Monthly Principal	Normal Payment	Additional Principal	Total Payment
1 _____	$ _____ +	(month 2) $ _____ =	$ _____
2 _____	$ _____ +	(month 4) $ _____ =	$ _____
3 _____	$ _____ +	(month 6) $ _____ =	$ _____
4 _____	$ _____ +	(month 8) $ _____ =	$ _____
5 _____	$ _____ +	(month 10) $ _____ =	$ _____
6 _____	$ _____ +	(month 12) $ _____ =	$ _____
7 _____	$ _____ +	(month 14) $ _____ =	$ _____
8 _____	$ _____ +	(month 16) $ _____ =	$ _____
9 _____	$ _____ +	(month 18) $ _____ =	$ _____
10 _____	$ _____ +	(month 20) $ _____ =	$ _____
11 _____	$ _____ +	(month 22) $ _____ =	$ _____
12 _____	$ _____ +	(month 24) $ _____ =	$ _____

Now, here is some great news: if you follow the payment schedule above for the next twelve months, you will have shortened your loan by not just one year, but two. Your principal reduction progressively gets larger every month, which is why your payment changes. If you want to keep things simple, take the total payment from month 6 and pay that amount all year long. The results will be virtually identical, but keep in mind you will still need to recalculate your payment amount every year to keep up.

Aside from paying your home off much sooner (which you won't get to enjoy until later), let's look at your realized wealth creation. Combine the Additional Principal payment amounts you made over the one-year period and enter the amount below:

Additional One-Year Principal Reduction: $ _____

PART THREE: WEALTH BUILDER ESSENTIALS

This is the additional amount of your home that you now own. Now let's look at the amount of wealth you protected. By being disciplined and taking this little extra step each month, you are greatly reducing the amount of money you will have to pay to get your home's deed in hand.

Look at your amortization chart and run the following calculation. Use the combined amount of your principal and interest payment (*not* the actual amount of your payment, which includes unavoidable taxes and insurance).

Accelerated Mortgage (One-Year, Wealth Saved)	
Principal and Interest Payment × 12 =	$_____
	−
Total Additional Principal Paid	$_____
	=
Total Wealth Saved	$_____

The Total Wealth Saved plus your Total Additional Principal Paid is all the wealth that you have protected using this method. Not only have you secured a larger portion of your house (via additional principal payments), but you've also avoided roughly a year's worth of interest payments ($7,450 or more in squandered wealth based on our $150,000 example home). So essentially your extra $184 monthly payment has saved you an additional $621 per month. That's not a bad return on investment.

The reason I promote this strategy is because (just like getting a 15-year mortgage) your home is paid off sooner, which saves you huge amounts of interest and makes you a true homeowner in half the time. It also allows flexibility in your monthly overhead should you have an emergency and have to skip paying the increased amount for a month or two (which results in additional financial security).

Also, with the wealth builder approach your payment starts low and consistently increases over time until you are eventually paying approximately twice as much. You may wonder, "How in the heck will I ever be able to afford that?" Herein lies the beauty of this method: your income will be growing and going up over time as your payment increases, so it won't necessarily be any more of a burden.

Let's look at the big picture to see the dramatic difference you can expect to achieve using this method. Go back to the amortization tool you are using. Enter your loan information and calculate the total principal and interest to pay off your loan as it stands today. If this is a new home you are considering purchasing, use the 30-year term for your loan length parameter. Then perform the same calculation based on paying your loan off in 15 years and enter both the numbers below.

Accelerated Mortgage Wealth Saved	
Total Paid for Current Loan (after 30 years):	$ _____
	-
Total Paid for Accelerated Payoff (after 15 years):	$ _____
	=
Total Wealth Saved:	$ _____

That's a large sum of money saved that otherwise would have been profit for a bank!

Fifteen Years Later

Now that you own your home outright, what are you going to do with the remaining 15 years that you would've been making payments? How about investing the money you would've paid towards your mortgage every month over the next 15 years? The picture would look like this (based on our $150,000 example, with an investment annual return of 10%):

Monthly Investment Amount: **$805.23**

Months to Contribute: **180**

Total Contributed to Investment: **$145,000**

Total Investment Value: **$337,000**

Add in the value of the example home (which would have a value of approximately $272,000 based on a 2% annual appreciation over the 30-year period). Your total wealth amassed via this prospect alone would be close to $609,000.

This approach differs from the advice many financial experts give, which is based on creating the maximum amount of wealth in the shortest period of time. Typically, advisors would advocate for investing the extra mortgage money at a 10% interest return, essentially leveraging the bank's money. The reasoning is, if you are only paying 5% interest on the bank's money, why rush to pay that off when you can get a 10% return by investing?

The reason the former method is superior is because both investing and carrying a mortgage are gambling. I want to minimize risk and keep my exposure low in case things go bad, especially since history proves they can and will. If you invested that principal overpayment instead over the first 15 years and then let it sit for the next 15 (continuing to pay off the example loan in 30 years) then at a 10% interest rate your total wealth created from investing would be about $614,000. Add in the value of the $272,000 home and you have created $886,000, or $277,000 more than the wealth builder scenario. The math on that one's a bit crazy and the increase is tempting but ultimately not worth the extra risk, and I'm going to explain why.

What happens if 15 years into your aggressive investment plan you only have your home half paid for and the economy takes a dive? The stock market could get cut in half like it did in 2009. That rosy picture could end up looking like this: your investment account after 15 years amassed a value of $147,000 but due to the recession is cut in half down to $73,500. Your home value (which has appreciated to $202,000) took a 30% hit because of the poor economy, and now has a value of $141,000. What's more is you still owe $115,000 on it! Your 15-year net value (based on the investments and your house) would total about $100,000. Doesn't seem too bad, right? On the other hand, if you had chosen to pay off your home you would be worth at least $41,000 more (thanks to having your $141,000 home paid for). This just shows one situation where if you had invested instead of paying off your home you would actually be in a far worse financial situation.

If for some reason you lost your job and you had to cash in your investments, you would likely have to pay taxes and possibly even penalties on that money. It would dramatically shrink the value of your investments and force you to use that money to cover house payments so you don't lose it to foreclosure. The result is that most of what you would pay is eaten by interest, destroying even more wealth. If you end up burning through all your money, you could end up putting your home equity and personal security at risk. The outcome could be disastrous, leaving you with bad credit and forcing you in to the rental market.

The Wealth Builder Lifestyle is a strategic system that will help keep you as financially strong as possible. Don't get overly greedy. Use the recommended strategy to get your home paid off as soon as you can. Even if you are already halfway done with paying it off, use the accelerated payoff method to shorten your remaining payoff by half.

NOTES :

_____

_____

_____

CONCLUSION

SUCCESSFULLY ACHIEVING GOALS

If you don't currently have specific goals set or you're not taking the actions necessary to reach them, your current habits (good or bad) are determining your goals for you. I'm going to give you four simple questions that if you continually ask yourself, will greatly increase your chances of not only meeting your goals, but exceeding them.

You can use this little acronym to help you remember them.
P.E.T.S (Plan, Effective, Tool, Status)

(P – Plan) Does this support my plan?

Any time you step outside the daily habits that are aligned with your overall goals, ask yourself, "Does this support my plan? Will taking this action move me closer to or further away from my goal?" This is applicable to any variation in your life. Ask it when you're deciding whether to go out to dinner, a movie, or on a vacation. Each action we take has a positive or negative effect on our life, so asking this question will help ensure you stay focused on the positives and avoid the negatives.

(E – Effective) Is this the most effective way?

When you do make a change outside your normal routine, perhaps you will find it's positive and for the best. However, take your consideration one step further. Ask, "Is this the most effective way to get the results I desire?" Consider all your options. If it's not, take the more effective alternative you come up with. We want momentum. We don't just want to do the bare minimum and get good results, we want to get the *best* results.

(T – Tool) Is there a tool that can help?

Often we think that what we know or currently think about is all there is. Break out of that mindset. Look outside your usual environment for tools that can help you get better results and make more informed decisions. This will help you excel beyond your current abilities. When it comes to wealth building, you need to actually **use** the tools in this program. Do not just read through them once. If you're going to buy a car or a luxury item, for example, use the tools within to refresh your thoughts and make sure you continually make the best decisions.

CONCLUSION
(S – Status) What is my status?

Ask yourself, "What is my status?" It's great to stay focused and effectively moving forward, but part of staying motivated is recognizing your growth. How much progress have you made? How much closer to your goal are you? Connect your focus and actions with your results so you can clearly see the benefits of your efforts and sacrifices.

Rewarding Results

Remember to use that fun money and reward yourself for good results. Part of sticking with any plan is rewarding yourself when you do stick with it. Don't underestimate the power of dangling a metaphorical carrot in front of yourself as motivation. If you have been diligent and successful in living the Wealth Builder Lifestyle, don't be afraid to make some temporary (but safe and well thought out) exceptions to the rules for a greater reward. Not only is doing so okay, but I actually *encourage* you to do this each time you achieve a substantial benchmark. Don't do it randomly—make the most of these larger rewards by setting your benchmarks and rewards in advance. Keep your plunder in proportion to your achievement. Say, for instance, you successfully pay off $10,000 in debt. Maybe after that you could set aside your debt reduction contributions until you save up $500 to take a weekend trip to some place you really love. Decide on your benchmarks and rewards early on, and then start planning immediately so that each positive step towards it is associated with being one step closer to whatever your reward is.

Have some fun with it. You can be focusing on multiple goals and rewards at the same time. Let's say that in five years when the house is paid off you're going to take a cruise to the Bahamas for your reward—no problem! Get some literature from your travel agent or the cruise line about the specific cruise you want to take. Start looking into and planning your trip with the expectation that you will achieve your goal on or before the target date so you can be on that cruise. Use something you really want that will motivate you and that you will really appreciate after all the hard work.

GRATITUDE AND CONTRIBUTION

When it comes to being truly wealthy, gratitude and contribution are powerful players. As you begin achieving your personal dreams, don't forget all the people and opportunities that made it all possible. Sure, you are the one working your butt off—and that is admirable—but nothing happens on behalf of oneself exclusively. Having an attitude of gratitude along with your material wealth will not only make you the admiration of others, but it will also fill you up on the inside, something money alone will never be able to do.

Pay it forward: contribute back to your community by sharing your wisdom and putting a percentage of your financial means into achieving something good. I think we all know about the unique needs of those around us, so it's less about the vehicle we choose to use and more about the impact. If we all donated our time and money to the same causes, many other great causes would end up neglected, slipping through the cracks and not getting the attention they need.

I personally think that if we all contributed a combination of our time, energy, and/or financial resources toward solving a problem or helping to fulfill a need that we are uniquely aware of, we could dramatically change the world for the better. It's easy for those who figure out the system of life to receive wealth in abundance, but if we don't give back we will be living a self-serving and unfulfilling life of greed. Not contributing defies the inherent values of humanity, which will internally take its toll and never allow complete fulfillment to those of us who skimp on giving back.

NOTES :

_____

_____

_____

_____

_____

_____

_____

MONEY MENTOR FOR KIDS

As parents, we all have a moral obligation to pass on good wealth building skills to our children. But how? Most parents I talk to are focused on learning to master wealth themselves, leaving their kids to pick up their own habits through watching others or through personal life experiences. Leaving them to fend for themselves may have merit, but leaving it up to chance is not a good way to set up our children for success.

I have included a simple wealth-mastery plan for parents to use with their children. This plan can be adapted to be utilized with very young children but in my opinion should be a must for children 10 years or older.

We severely underestimate our children's learning abilities, especially when it comes to money. We have christened money as "adult talk," therefore failing to proactively make efforts to help our kids understand money at higher levels. What's more is we've often gone out of our way to keep them from seeing our relevant struggles and successes. We think we are doing them a favor by not burdening them with concerns about money management. Kids were born to learn—let them learn! A hard time can be one of the most beneficial learning experiences a child can have.

Program Outline

I hope that if you have kids this simple program can work as well for yours as it did for mine. In the following pages you will find a Paycheck Calculator (timecard), this is used to track their daily performance. Each chore has a daily monetary value. You will decide each chore and how much each is worth. Yes, you will be paying your kids to perform—it's a lot like the real world, so they better get used to it!

Here is the deal: you are going to be turning over financial responsibility to them for some key expenses, such as things they want and are motivated to get. Their pay should not be akin to the small allowance most people give their children. Rather, this should be a decent sum of money. You will be turning over financial control for things like their personal expenses, fun money, and even some investment funds.

CONCLUSION

In the following worksheet, divide the total pay you will be putting on the table each week by seven and enter that amount for the Total Daily Pay. Then divide that amount by the total Number of Jobs you will have for them to do (which will determine the daily pay rate per job).

Per Job Pay Rate (Money Mentor)			
Total Weekly Pay	Total Daily Pay	Number of Jobs	Pay Rate Per Job
$_____ ÷ 7 =	$_____	÷ _____ =	$_____

You'll also want to choose jobs that will help them establish good lifelong habits. Think of what skills you want your children to make habitual that will have lasting value. The habits that allow them to earn money today will become a natural part of their lives and remain with them long after the paychecks from you stop.

NOTES :

_____
_____
_____
_____
_____
_____
_____
_____
_____
_____
_____
_____
_____
_____
_____
_____

MONEY MENTOR FOR KIDS

This following worksheet should be posted where everyone can see it, like on the refrigerator. As a part of their jobs, your kids are responsible for filling this out daily (preferably after each job is completed). You may give them some reminders when you first start the program, but then you should leave it up to them to be responsible for completing it or missing a portion of their pay. No, it is not mean. If you stand by your rules, they won't miss getting paid often. Soon enough you'll find that they've created a great habit.

Paycheck Calculator (Money Mentor)								
Job, Task, or Chore	Saturday	Sunday	Monday	Tuesday	Wednesday	Thursday	Friday	Total
_____								
_____								
_____								
_____								
_____								
_____								
_____								
				Total Jobs Completed				_____
								×
				Pay Per Successfully Completed Job				$_____
								=
				Total Weekly Paycheck				$_____

They will make mistakes—it's not only likely, it's to be expected. When they do, let them experience the consequences. The consequences of our mistakes are how we learn: all successful people have made many mistakes and learned from them. If you always bail your kids out, they won't learn to be responsible adults (and it will be no fault of their own).

CONCLUSION

Just like with our money, there are rules for how their money is allocated and to be spent. This will involve some oversight on your part. Here is how their overall pay should be allocated.

Business Investments

Yep, that's right—business investments. Just like with the Wealth Builder Lifestyle, your kid's contributions can be dumped in to a growth investment account if you so choose. I on the other hand wanted my kids to learn the art of negotiation, how to evaluate values of different assets, and to have the opportunity to increase the value of their money through compounding means.

If you choose the same they could, for example, run a car wash. Or, they could buy and sell stuff from garage sales, Craigslist, or E-bay. You will have to establish the overall rules for that type of activity, but however you do it you want to make it clear that their money is their working capital to buy materials, products, or advertising. This can be a great hobby as well as a fabulous learning experience. Take a little time to show them how to determine the value of items, what it will cost to market, calculate the expenses of shipping (if applicable), and determine their profit margins (sale price minus total cost of sale).

Growth Investments

This money should be utilized in one of two ways. They can either put it in to a savings account of their own (in which case you would provide a 10% annual return on their money), or (preferably) you could put it in to your online trading account and setup a portfolio of their own so that they can watch their money grow. As they get older, let them research different funds or stocks and move their money around. The main thing is they need to be able to see the value of their investment account because you want them to be totally aware of how money grows.

Personal Expenses

This is the money you would normally spend on them for clothes, school supplies, personal products, and so on. This money should be kept in a savings account or in your possession (until they are old enough to take care of it), but they should be the ones tracking and maintaining the balance. They will take over responsibility for buying their clothes and other necessary items. If they have a phone, for example, you could put the money for it in this category and let them pay it directly. Who knows? Maybe they will want to downgrade to a cheaper plan.

The goal is to connect our children with the value of money while they are in their peak learning years. Gone will be the days of blowing a fortune on one trendy outfit. That type of money management will force them to have to wear their old clothes every other day of the week.

Fun Money

Last but not least is fun money. You should let them have 100% full control of this money with no restrictions—well, that is, outside of maybe just the following one. The rule is that you cannot eat your money, which means no buying candy, soda, or other junk food with it. Outside of that they can go to the movies, buy toys, whatever they want. They get this money in cold hard cash every Saturday. This works out well because when they don't have the money to go do something with their friends it is all on them. This will encourage them to keep a little stash set aside for those fun times, while building discipline and forming good financial habits. Empowering your kids by putting them in charge of their money is a great opportunity for them to learn. If you follow these rules and don't cave when they come up short, you will be amazed at how well they learn to do on their own.

Income Allocations

How you choose to allocate the percentage of their total pay that goes towards each category is up to you. You need to decide what works and will fit your goals. What I chose to do was set aside 25% for fun money, 40% for personal expenses, 20% for growth investments, and 15% for business investments. If they miss their income-earning opportunities, make sure they still stick to the allocated percentages strictly—no robbing Peter to pay Paul! If they have to go a month without having a phone, so be it. Letting them change their allocations would just teach them that they don't have to have good financial habits and can get the reward without the responsibility of performing.

NOTES :

_____

_____

_____

_____

_____

CONCLUSION

Here is a tool you can use to easily calculate their weekly paycheck allocations. I would advise that you let them start calculating their own paychecks and allocations as soon as they are capable of it because it will help build their money calculating skills.

Paycheck Distribution (Money Mentor)			
Pay Allocations	Total Weekly Pay Earned	Percentage of Pay	Category Total
Business Investments	$_____	× _____% =	$_____
Growth Investments		× _____% =	$_____
Personal Money		× _____% =	$_____
Fun Money		× _____% =	$_____

NOTES :

___
___
___
___
___
___
___
___
___
___
___
___

Just like adults, they need to be aware of and track their results so they can see the effects of their actions. To achieve this, they need to be aware of their total net worth. For my kids this was a big deal because as their net worth grew they developed a sense of pride about what they were accomplishing. This became a topic that they were all too happy to talk about, which resulted in them getting a lot of positive feedback.

Setup a time once a month to check their accounts and update the following net worth statement. It is good to do this monthly with kids as their attention spans are so short. The frequent revisits will help keep them focused through repetition. Let them do as much of this as they can on their own as soon as possible.

Net Worth Evaluator (Money Mentor)		Date ___/___/_____	
Asset	Value	Liability	Value
Business Investments	$_____	Loans	$_____
Growth Investments	$_____	Other Debts	$_____
Personal Money	$_____	Total Liabilities	$_____
Fun Money	$_____		
Other Cash	$_____		
Personal Property		Net Worth	
_____	$_____	Total Assets	$_____
_____	$_____	Total Liabilities	$_____
_____	$_____	Total Net Worth	$_____
_____	$_____	(net worth = assets – liabilities)	
_____	$_____	*"You can choose to live the habits of the lifestyles of the rich and famous or the habits of the poor and destitute. You decide!"*	
Total Assets	$_____		

CONCLUSION

Here is one more form that you may want to use to track their monthly income. It can be a good historical reference so they can see their track record over time.

Monthly Income (Money Mentor)	
Month _____ Year _____	Weekly Income
Week One	$_____
Week Two	$_____
Week Three	$_____
Week Four	$_____
Week Five	$_____
Total Monthly Income	$_____

You may want to get a three ring binder or other folder that they can use to keep their records in. This way they can look back over the years and see how they amassed so much wealth. If you start them on this program early, by the time they are ready to buy a car they will be able to purchase it with their own money. They will also have a sense of pride that is unimaginable and take much better care of it than they would if you had bought it for them.

If you choose to try this simple system with your kids, I think you will be amazed with the results, just like I was. Sure, it will be a little bit of work, but I promise you it will be well worth it in the end. Oddly enough, teaching is one of the best ways to learn, so while you are teaching them you will also be sharpening your own skills. This will also be a great bonding experience and let's face it: what loving parent wouldn't want a great bonding experience?

NOTES :

_____
_____
_____
_____
_____

CLOSING THOUGHTS

Without a doubt, living a Wealth Builder Lifestyle will empower you to consistently create wealth. How successful you are in the transition from where you are to a true wealth builder will be dictated by your dedication to mastering your personal finances.

If there is one thing you take away from this, I hope you learn *how* to think about money, not *what* to think. This program has a pretty formal outline of how to manage your finances to build wealth, however, there is no exact strategy that will fit everyone and be the most effective approach to achieve their goals.

This program is filled with time-tested principles that work. How you can best use them to the fullest extent comes down to your ability to think through your application and exact strategy.

We all have the God-given ability to become good thinkers. Your ability to think intelligently is not predetermined. By working through this program, you have taken a huge step towards strengthening your financial skills and decision-making abilities. This should not be the end, just part of your continuous journey in improving your knowledge. The one sure thing is that wealth and success will always follow the informed thinkers.

We live in a world that is changing faster than any time in history. Today's rapid pace will affect your wealth strategy, lifestyle, and almost every aspect of your life. I continually focus on learning the latest strategies of what works in all aspects of life and I encourage you to do the same. Setup a plan for constant improvement and you will always thrive and prosper to the best of your abilities.

The world will give you what you deserve, so make the most of your abilities and leave the struggling to the lazy and slothful.

For electronic copies of the worksheets in this book, please go to www.WealthBuilderLifestyle.com/tools.

Live Rich and Die Wealthy

ABOUT THE AUTHOR

Daniel Hartjoy is the founder of Methods For Mastery, Inc. and the author of multiple books dedicated to helping people break through their personal barriers and achieve their ultimate dreams. He is well known for his commitment to helping others reach their highest levels of performance and personal success. His ability to see the best in every person and situation is legendary. Through the use of a philanthropist approach to sharing his abundance of life changing strategies, he is dedicated to impacting a much broader spectrum of humanity. One of his primary objectives is to reach out to those who typically fall through the cracks and get left behind.

Having come from humble beginnings with no college education, he has used his unique approaches to take his income from $8 an hour, to earning over $100,000 in a single month. He has worked his way up through the corporate world smashing through boundaries his education and background said he couldn't cross. He has also started multiple companies and broke and rewrote the rules that businesses are supposed to operate under, leading to phenomenal growth in record time. This includes launching an out of state company he would manage remotely that would go from nothing to almost $3,000,000 in revenue the first year, with a profit margin in excess of 30%. It was through these experiences he realized that life has so much more to offer us than what we ask of it. If someone can break free of their false beliefs of what they expect from and hope to achieve in life, their world can be changed forever. Through the use of his books, live events and personal coaching he continues to make his life changing message and strategies available around the globe.

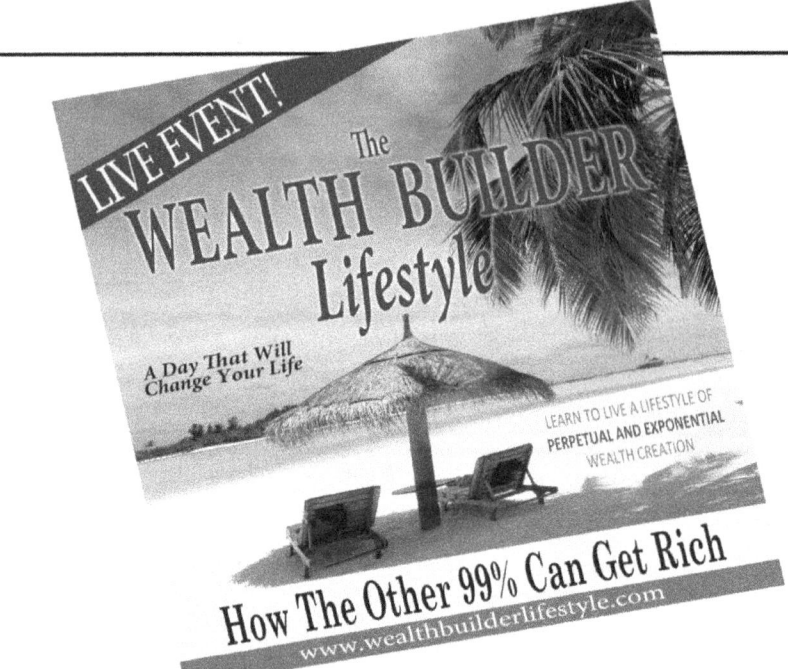

JOIN US LIVE!

Congratulations!
You have already taken more action towards attaining your dreams than most ever will. I invite you to continue your journey and join us for the Wealth Builder Lifestyle LIVE EVENT. If you really want to make what you have already started to learn really stick and become a deeply engrained part of your life, then attending the live event is your next step. Most people retain about 10% of what they read in a book, through the live event format we have the ability to use advanced training technologies that can dramatically increase your level of retention. This is an amazing experience and a great way to continue your financial education. Scan the QR Code or email us at the address below to learn more and recieve your exclusive ticket offer.

To Get Your Promotional Tickets
Email: promotions@wealthbuilderlifestyle.com

COMING SOON
December - 2014

The
WEALTH BUILDER
Lifestyle 2.0

The Millionaire Blueprint

In this highly anticipated follow up to The Wealth Builder Lifestyle: How The Other 99% Can Get Rich book, you'll learn to create your own personalized Millionaire Blueprint. This will be your wealth creation action plan from now until you retire. Not only will you create a detailed plan of action but the wealth forcaster will allow you to see just how much wealth you can expect to obtain during your lifetime if you follow your blueprint.

Gone will be the days of working a lifetime only to find out you came up short of your retirement financial needs. If your blueprint doesn't have the potential to reach your goals, change it now!

Don't take Daniel Hartjoy's claim "anyone can retire a millionaire regardless of their income" on his word, let him show you how it's possible in black and white detail.

Included he will also share his investing 202 strategies for rapidly creating more wealth. By now you should know these will not be get rich quick schemes but genuine and powerful wealth building techniques.

www.ingramcontent.com/pod-product-compliance
Lightning Source LLC
Chambersburg PA
CBHW081455040426
42446CB00016B/3247